Tests

Texts and Tests

TEACHING STUDY SKILLS ACROSS CONTENT AREAS

Rona F. Flippo

Kaneland Middle School
1N137 Meredith Rd.
Maple Park, IL 60151

Heinemann
Portsmouth, NH

Heinemann

A division of Reed Elsevier Inc.

361 Hanover Street

Portsmouth, NH 03801-3912

www.heinemann.com

Offices and agents throughout the world

© 2004 by Rona F. Flippo

The author and publisher wish to thank those who have generously given permission to reprint borrowed material:

Figures 3–1, 3–4, 3–6 developed and adapted from Karen D. Wood, Diane Lapp, and James Flood (1992). *Guiding Readers Through Text: A Review of Study Guides.* Used by permission of the International Reading Association.

Figure 3–2 and 3–5 developed and adapted from Karen D. Wood (1988), "Guiding Students Through Informational Text" in *The Reading Teacher,* 4(9). Used by permission of the International Reading Association.

Figure 3–3 developed and adapted from F. A. Duffelmeyer, D. D. Baum, and D. J. Merkley (1987), "Maximizing Reader-Text Confrontation with an Extended Anticipation Guide" in *Journal of Reading,* 31. Used by permission of the International Reading Association.

Figure 4–2 from R. F. Flippo and C. R. Frounfelker, III, "Teach Map Reading Through Self Assessment" in *The Reading Teacher,* 42(3). Copyright © 1988 by the International Reading Association. Reprinted by permission of Rona F. Flippo and the International Reading Association.

Library of Congress Cataloging-in-Publication Data

Flippo, Rona F.

    Texts and tests : teaching study skills across content areas / Rona F. Flippo.

      p. cm.

    Includes bibliographical references.

    ISBN 0-325-00491-9 (alk. paper)

    1. Study skills.   2. Content area reading. I. Title.

LB1601 .F55 2004

371.3′028′1—dc22   2003022903

Editor: Lois Bridges

Production coordinator: Sonja S. Chapman

Production service: Denise A. Botelho

Cover design: Night & Day Design

Typesetter: Publishers' Design and Production Services, Inc.

Manufacturing: Steve Bernier

Printed in the United States of America on acid-free paper

08 07 06 05 04   RRD   1 2 3 4 5

To Elena Graham, our inquisitive and clever granddaughter, who uses each encounter with text to interact, learn, and enjoy. Your delight in learning and books thrills us. We love you, and we are so proud of the learner you are.

From Grandma (Dama) and Grandpa (Papa)

Elena Graham at eighteen months with author (Grandma)...

...reading and studying a book.

...interacting and learning from a book.

Photos by Tyler Fox (Grandpa)

Contents

Acknowledgments

First of all, I am proud to acknowledge the excellent contributions of three of my graduate students to this book. They are listed here in alphabetical order, but each made equal contributions, providing ideas for Reflection Activities, "Try It Out" Activities, technology assignments, and the Studying and Learning Strategies: Teaching and Performance Grid. Thank you for your professional contributions to this work, Candace D. Fournier, Jeffrey P. Maider, and Mara Safer.

Thanks, too, to my typist, Ron Elbert, whose editorial expertise is beyond compare. To my husband, Tyler Fox, whose support and confidence are most important to continuing my ongoing work. To my daughter, Tara Flippo, whose love is always nurturing. To my son, Todd Graham and his wife Jenne, who have provided me with the most wonderful inspiration of all, my granddaughter Elena. Delight in being with her; watching her learn, grow, and interact with books; and her love for life and learning all new things are the greatest joy. I also thank my husband, Tyler, for being a wonderful grandpa (Papa) and for the great pictures he always takes of Elena—several of which are included at the beginning of this book.

Finally, I wish to thank my fabulous editor at Heinemann, Lois Bridges, for recognizing the need for this book and the Graduate Studies Office at Fitchburg State College for providing some financial support for its typing.

Introduction

This book has been developed especially for classroom teachers of students in first through eighth grade as a "primer" to strategies for studying and learning from text. Its purpose is to provide a no-nonsense, nuts-and-bolts guide to specific strategies and activities that teachers can use with their students in order to help them learn from text materials used in the classroom. The focus of these strategies is for students to develop and hone efficient and effective study and learning skills to further their independence as learners.

This book presents a rationale and many ideas and examples for teaching and developing elementary grade as well as middle school students' study-learning skills and strategies. "Learning how to learn" is the goal of all schooling. When teachers and students are aware of the study-learning tasks, the skills and strategies involved, and the methods and expectations regarding assessment and performance, "knowing how to learn" can become a reality. Even when the goal is clearly to develop students' independence, students still need teacher demonstration, guidance, and support.

Most of the content and teaching examples in this book have been developed with materials and curriculum in mind for grades 2, 3, and 4 and up through grades 5 and 6. My rationale is that interested teachers of first grade can adjust the difficulty of the tasks and content materials down for their students and teachers of grades 7 and 8 can easily adjust the tasks and content as appropriate to their students and curriculum. The goal has been to provide some concrete examples of what the study-learning skill and strategy tasks and activities might actually look like. Teachers of students in grades 1 through 8 are in the best position to design their own activities, following these examples, with their own students, curriculum, materials, and learning objectives.

Teachers can use many of the same good teaching techniques that they already use to enhance and develop reading, writing, thinking, and learning across the curriculum. The use of demonstration, modeling, and scaffolding is especially endorsed. Additionally, the teaching techniques of scaffolded reading experiences, use of study guides, and fading are presented as techniques that can be used to enhance study-learning. Mrs. Argueta, a fourth-grade teacher, is introduced in this book, and her study-reading assignment for students is used to illustrate how to do meaningful study-learning work. In addition, several study-learning examples of prereading, during-reading, and postreading activities and an assortment of study guides for use with elementary to middle school students are provided.

Various study-learning skills and strategies, as well as important student organizational skills, are identified and described in this text. Many specialized study-learning skills and strategies also are identified and discussed. Teachers will note that I use expository texts for my examples throughout this book. This is because most of the studying and learning that students are required to do in school is from expository (content) texts. Additionally, although I believe that use of multiple texts is a good idea and should be encouraged, in many of my examples and explanations, particularly in the chapters on study guides and strategy systems, you will note that I focus on one-text assignments. This is because study guides and strategy systems were specifically developed by teachers and researchers to help students learn the information from a *particular* textbook reading in their assigned science, social studies, or other content textbooks.

Finally, several specific strategy systems for reading, studying, and learning from text are presented, and the need to embed the teaching of study-learning skills and strategies in authentic active content learning and assignments designed for your particular students is reiterated. Students must view study-learning activities as purposeful, helpful, and rewarding in order to benefit. Otherwise, they could be viewed as exercises that take away from the time students really need to get their "real work" done.

A "Teaching and Performance" grid that names the included studying and learning strategies in alphabetical order across the various categories and chapters is displayed at the beginning of this book. This grid indicates the purposes of the strategies and activities by identifying which ones reinforce or involve performance of the skills of reading, summarizing, outlining, researching, report writing, response writing, discussing, and preparing for objective or essay tests. It should be noted that some of the study-learning strategies put all or many of these skills in practice. This grid provides an overview for teachers and information about the strategies that could be very helpful for performance assessment purposes. (Considerations of space did not permit inclusion of all the possible skills that these strategies involve.)

Additionally, each chapter has Reflection Activities to keep you engaged. Feel free to skip over them if they distract you or if you don't have time for them. Also, "Try It Out" Activities are provided at the end of each chapter, as well as at the end of this book. These activities have been designed to engage your students and keep them actively involved in the study-learning process. You are free to pick and choose from them, and better still, to create your own. Finally, an appendix of the most frequently used studying and learning forms is provided. Teachers are *invited* and given permission to copy them, use them as is, or adapt them to fit their particular needs, assignments, and situations.

Main Ideas

- "Learning how to learn" should be the main goal of schooling.
- Study-learning skills and strategies can be introduced in the early elementary grades and continued throughout the elementary and middle school years.
- It is important for students and teachers to be aware of study-learning tasks, skills, and strategies that will be needed and of how learning and performance will be evaluated.
- Many tried and true teaching strategies are especially suited for the study-learning development of students: demonstration, modeling, scaffolding, fading, and use of many different study guides.
- Study-learning skills and strategies instruction should be embedded in the regular content instruction of the classroom.

- Study-learning assignments, tasks, and activities should be motivating and intrinsically rewarding for students.
- Reference and research skills include the use of dictionaries, encyclopedias, library resources, and the Internet to locate and assemble information.
- Organizational skills include the use of outlining, underlining and student glossing, and note taking and note making.
- Specialized study-learning skills include using parts of textbooks to find information, reading graphically displayed information, skimming and scanning, adjusting reading rate, and test-preparation and test-taking skills.
- Test-preparation and test-taking skills are particularly important and should be developed over time from the elementary through middle school grades.
- Strategy systems for reading, studying, and learning from texts can be used with and demonstrated to students as additional tools for learning how to learn. These include: K-W-L, Reciprocal Teaching and Learning, Predict-Test-Conclude, Think-Alouds, PORPE, REAP, SQ3R, PARS, SIP, RIPS, and Inference Awareness.

The traditional emphasis of literacy instruction in elementary through middle school years has tended to focus on word identification, comprehension, and writing skills. However, literacy development and learning involve much more than just developing these traditional, but necessary, skills. McKenna and Robinson (2002) have indicated that the research on the psychology of learning suggests that students must be actively engaged with the content we expect them to learn in order to actually learn it. As students move from the early grades toward and into the upper grades, they will be confronted with more and more complex study and learning demands. Teachers of first graders through eighth graders certainly want their students to have the skills and strategies to deal with these increasing demands. But what can teachers really do to help their students meet these learning tasks and demands? This book will present information that will answer this and other questions related to studying and learning from texts and assignments. I hope you will find it useful in developing your students' independence as learners.

Learning How to Learn

Helping students learn how to learn should really be the main goal of schooling. Anyone who has actually taught in a school knows that teachers can never begin to teach *everything*. *Everything* is too much! Instead, teachers endeavor to create an environment that enables students to eventually learn by themselves as needed. In that way, when students are expected to do independent work in school, and even when they are not in school, they will be able to direct their own learning when necessary or at their own discretion. However, in order to learn how to learn, our students first need ample opportunity to practice and be mentored while under our guidance. Study skills are tools that, when combined with reading, writing, and thinking skills and strategies, equip students for learning how to learn. Just as teachers devote time to reading and writing instruction in meaningful situations, they must also devote time to teaching students how to learn in meaningful situations. The key is for learners to be interested, motivated, actively engaged, able to adapt to the task and text, and able to apply the strategies that are needed for each occasion. Turner and Paris (1995) have indicated that "If students are to be motivated readers and writers, we must give them the tools and the reasons to read and write and allow them to discover the many paths to literacy—paths that fit the diverse goals, purposes, interests, and social needs of children" (p. 672).

Anderson and Armbruster (1984) noted that studying is a special form of reading. That it differs from other forms of reading is evident because students are expected "to study and learn" specific information that they will have to discuss or on which they will be tested. Students have to visualize the outcomes of studying as a function of the interaction between stated and processing variables. *Stated variables* relate to the status of the student and the material to be studied. Student elements include such variables as knowledge of the criterion task, knowledge of the content in the material to be studied, and interest and motivation. Text elements are features that affect the readability of the material, such as content and organization. *Processing variables* are concerned with getting information from the printed page through the students' thought processes. These processing variables include the initial focusing of attention, subsequent encoding of information, long- and short-term memory storing, and retrieving of the information.

Learning how to learn can be just as complex a task for students as learning to read. Although it is a teacher's responsibility to help students learn how to learn, it is the students' responsibility as well. "Knowing how to learn" can become the goal for both teachers and students when both are aware of the tasks and skill and strategy demands involved.

Reflection Activity 1.1

In your own words, what does learning how to learn involve? How does a curriculum that emphasizes learning how to learn fit in with your current beliefs, experiences, and classroom work? What could you share with other teachers to convince them of the importance of learning how to learn?

Studying and Learning Considerations

Studying and learning involve task awareness, strategy awareness, and awareness of how to think about and monitor learning and performance (Anderson and Armbruster 1984; Baker and Brown 1984; Wade and Reynolds 1989). This involves being metacognitively aware. Just as students' awareness in these areas is important to studying and learning, teachers' awareness is also vitally important. In the sections that follow, each of these areas is discussed, and examples are given of both the teacher's and students' roles in teaching and learning how to learn.

Awareness of the Study-Learning Task

Knowing and understanding what is expected, or what the actual task is, is critical to being able to perform or do the task (Anderson and Armbruster 1984). For example, if students are expected to know certain information for a test, they must be aware of what that information is and how they will be tested on it (Flippo 2000). Here is another example: If students are expected to write a report, they must be aware of what should be included in the report, the format and other requirements for the report, and how it will be evaluated. Clearly, if a person is to perform satisfactorily on a task assigned by someone else, the assigner must provide the criteria for the task and the guidelines that will be used to evaluate the success of the task. Both the assigner and assignee have certain roles and responsibilities if performance of the task is to be satisfactorily completed.

Teacher's Role

As teachers, we can basically make any educationally sound learning or study assignments we elect to make. However, two important considerations must be 1) *have we analyzed what is required of students to complete the assignment?* and 2) *do the students have a clear idea of the purpose(s) and guidelines for the assignment and the criteria that will be used to evaluate performance of or on it?*

The assignment analysis sheet, as depicted in Figure 1–1, provides you with guidance and a procedure to analyze the study and learning strategies students will need to have or use for assignments you give them. Additionally, the reflection questions in Figure 1–1 should help you delineate guidelines or criteria to go with your assignments.

To illustrate how the assignment analysis sheet can be used, see Figure 1–2. In this figure, Mrs. Argueta has analyzed the study skills and strategies her fourth-grade students will need to complete their first research paper. As you can see, a lot of independent work is involved. How can Mrs. Argueta guide students and help them successfully fulfill their roles as learners?

Students' Role

When the teacher has explicitly made the study or learning assignment and purpose clear, students are in a better position to complete the task. Even so, students have their own roles and obligations concerning their learning and the completion of assignments. Some "learning to learn helpers" that can be used to clarify the task at hand and to help your students understand what is expected of them are as follows:

- Students should be encouraged to ask the teacher for clarification of any aspect of the assignment that they are unsure of or do not understand.
- Students should be encouraged to ask the teacher to show them a sample of what a successfully completed assignment might look like and/or to model some of the study skills and strategies involved.
- Students should be encouraged to discuss the assignment and criteria with other students when they feel that it would be helpful.
- Students should be encouraged to ask older peers, adults in school, their family, or community for advice and suggestions if they feel that it would be helpful (e.g., the school or community librarian might have some research advice to offer).
- Students should be encouraged to internalize the purpose for the assignment and make the assignment and the work involved "their own." If students view the purpose of the assignment as "authentic," this will more easily happen. (See the following example of how

Figure 1–1   Assignment analysis sheet

Assignment Analysis Sheet

1. Specific assignment or learning: _____
_____
_____
_____

2. Authentic purpose(s) for assignment or learning: _____
_____
_____
_____

3. Steps students will need to take in order to complete this assignment and learning: _____
_____
_____
_____
_____

4. Specific study skills and strategies needed to complete each step: _____
_____
_____
_____
_____

5. How this assignment or learning will be evaluated: _____
_____
_____
_____
_____

6. What is my exact criteria and requirements for this assignment or learning? _____
_____
_____
_____
_____
_____
_____

Assignment Analysis Sheet

1. Specific assignment or learning: _Students will research, develop, and write their "first" research paper on self-selected topics related to our integrated unit on rainforests._

2. Authentic purpose(s) for assignment or learning: _In order for all students to learn as much about rainforests as possible, individual students will select the aspects they find most interesting, research them, write reports, and share their reports with the class._

3. Steps students will need to take in order to complete this assignment and learning: _(a) Brainstorm possible topics of interest, consider them, select one, and plan what they want to research. (b) Go to library, research topic, write notes, and make a list of print and electronic sources. (c) Using the Internet, go online and find at least one rainforest specific Website and review and research the information pertinent to students' specific topics. (d) Write report and bibliography from notes. (e) Edit report and bib. with help of writing group, and publish report. (f) Gather any pictures or artifacts to go with report. If possible, use a scanner to insert a photo with the report or download an image from a Website to embed in the report. (g) Orally share with class._

4. Specific study skills and strategies needed to complete each step: _(a) Narrowing down a topic. (b) Planning and organizational skills. (c) Library reference and research skills—both print and electronic (using cataloguing systems, finding materials, using references to research). (d) Skimming and scanning, adjusting rate as necessary, using graphic information (tables, graphs, maps). (e) Note-taking from text skills. (f) Organizing notes and outlining information. (g) Summarizing. (h) Report writing. (i) Editing skills (including use of dictionary). (j) Oral reporting/sharing._

5. How this assignment or learning will be evaluated: _• Students library and Web research activities will be evaluated by their participation and success at finding material on topic. • Students reports and bibliography will be evaluated by their successful coverage of their topiocs and listings of materials used. • Students sharing will be evaluated by their publication of their reports and participation in oral sharing of their reports._

6. What is my exact criteria and requirements for this assignment or learning? _(a) Select a topic related to rainforests. (b) Find and use at least 4 library sources and 1 Website to get information on the topic. (c) Take notes from at least 4 different library sources and 1 Website. (d) Write a report that is at least 3 pages long. (e) Include at least 4 library references (print and electronic references) and at least 1 Website in the bibliography, according to format provided for books, newspapers, magazines, encyclopedias (print or CD-ROM), and the Internet. (f) Publish and orally share report (artifacts and pictures are nice, but optional)._

one fourth-grade student, Carmen, has internalized Mrs. Argueta's research paper assignment.)

Carmen understands that Mrs. Argueta wants each student to select the most interesting aspect of their integrated unit on rainforests, do library and Internet research on that aspect, and then write a report on it. At first Carmen was a little overwhelmed by the assignment, but after she asked lots of questions and talked and brainstormed with other students, she felt better and began to look forward to the assignment. Carmen is very interested in snakes and other reptiles, and she now knows that she can do her research and report on the more common snakes and reptiles found in the different rainforests of the world. Because Mrs. Argueta told the students that they may use pictures and artifacts when they share their reports, Carmen is planning to share photos and some samples she has of how snakes shed their skins, but first she must do research and find out whether the snakes in rainforests shed their skins. This will be fun for Carmen because she is highly motivated to pursue this area of study. Her understanding of the assignment and her motivation and internalization of the assignment are a very good beginning toward her satisfactory completion of the assignment. However, the next considerations, awareness of the skills and the strategies to use to complete the assignment, are equally important.

Awareness of the Skills and Strategies to Use

As we have seen in Figures 1–1 and 1–2, awareness of the study-learning task/assignment is different from awareness of the skills and strategies necessary to complete the assignment. Knowing the necessary skills and strategies and how to apply them to the study-learning task at hand involves both teacher and student responsibilities.

Teacher's Role

For every assignment we give students, teachers must be aware of the skills and strategies that students will need to complete the task. This involves first a delineation of the steps students must take to complete the task (see number 3 on Figures 1–1 and 1–2) and then an analysis of the specific study skills and strategies needed to complete each step (see number 4 on Figures 1–1 and 1–2). *Teachers must next decide whether students in their classroom have or know how to use the necessary study skills and strategies.* One of the best ways to determine this is by observing students do their usual classroom work. If teachers want to be systematic about these observations, they can do so by recording their findings on a simple class list or grid over a period of time, noting individual students' skill and strategy abilities and use. For an idea of what this might look like, see Figure 1–3.

It now seems opportune to differentiate between skills and strategies. Dole et al. (1991) indicated that *strategies* imply an awareness or reflection on what we do while we are learning; *skills* imply a more automatic response to learning (p. 242). Paris, Wasik, and Turner (1991) proposed that a developing skill can become a strategy when it is intentionally used. Flippo (2002, 2003) has indicated that study skills involve the ability to perform a learning-related task, and that the use of many study skills used together can form a strategy. Flippo (2003) has defined strategies as being the way we go about working out problems and that strategy instruction involves helping students develop and become aware of the strategies they use (p. 372).

If a teacher observes that some students lack the necessary study skills and strategies to do an assignment, the teacher's responsibility is to model and teach these skills. However, it is important to keep in mind that good study skill and strategy instruction is embedded rather than isolated instruction (Ruddell 2002, p. 261). In other words, study skill and strategy instruction, like reading and writing instruction, needs to be part of the larger instruction in your classroom. Children and older students will learn study skills when you develop opportunities to present them within the broader context of your curriculum (i.e., as part of reading the social studies chapter, as part of studying for the science quiz, etc.).

Students' Role

Students often have a lot to do in order to satisfactorily complete a given assignment. For example, to complete Mrs. Argueta's research paper assignment, take another look at Figure 1–2, number 3, to see what the fourth graders must do. Such tasks can sometimes be overwhelming for

Figure 1–3   Study skills and strategies checklist

Students' names:	Planning and organizing	Library and Internet research	Skimming and scanning	Adjusting rate	Using graphic information	Note taking	Outlining	Summarizing	Report writing	Editing	Using dictionary	Oral reporting	Notes:

Above the table, spanning the skill columns: **Study Skills and Strategies** an elementary- or middle-school-age student. In fact, many high school (Alvermann and Phelps 2002; Zemelman and Daniels 1988) and even college students (Allgood et al. 2000) are often overwhelmed by this type of assignment. However, when elementary-age students are guided and instructed on doing such assignments, they can be successful. Various reading educators have pointed out the importance of starting study and learning skills development at an early age by engaging elementary students in real study and inquiry activities (e.g., Flippo and Borthwick 1982; Hoyt 2002; Moore et al. 2003; Robb 2003).

To guide your students, to keep them from feeling overwhelmed, and to help them satisfactorily complete their study-learning tasks, encourage their planning and organizing activities. See the "think-through" sheets I have developed and provided for this purpose in Figures 1–4 and 1–5. These will give you some ideas to help guide your students. You may want to combine these sheets. You can also design your own "think-through" and other planning and organizing activities and skill-awareness sheets to fit your own instructional purposes.

Students also need to feel that they have enough time to complete the study-learning task. Your encouragement, belief in your students' abilities to successfully do the assigned task, and your students' motivation for completing the task will all contribute to your students' potential for success (e.g., see Cramer and Castle 1994; Dwyer and Dwyer 1994; Good and Brophy 1978; Guthrie 1994).

Sometimes students will need your help to understand how to perform and use necessary study skills and strategies. As can be seen in Figure 1–5, students need to know that they can come to you for help and guidance. Various teaching strategies, for example, modeling, scaffolding, and fading, can be used to provide this assistance and will be explained, along with study skill and strategy examples, later in this book. Additionally, specific information on a variety of study-learning skills and strategies are also provided.

Awareness of How to Monitor Learning and Performance

Ongoing evaluation and overall performance evaluation are an important part of studying and learning. Teachers must know how to monitor and assess students' work and success with the learning task. Students

Figure 1–4　Think-through "to do" sheet

Think-Through "To Do" Sheet	
What I have to do:	Check when it is done:
The order I should do it in:	
When I should do it:	

must also know how to self-monitor and evaluate their own learning and performance (Alvermann and Phelps 2002). This monitoring and assessment on the part of both the teacher and the students involves reflection and thinking. This reflection and thinking involves students' metacognitive strategies and control. Students with metacognitive control can use their learning strategies and skills as tools (Paris and Winograd 1990). Their self-regulated assessment and learning will help them accomplish academic goals and tasks (Borkowski et al. 1990). Moore et al. (2003) emphasized that self-monitoring and self-regulating learners plan to use strategies appropriate to specific learning tasks, check on their progress, and make adjustments as needed.

Figure 1–5	Think-through "how to do" sheet	
Think-Through "How To Do" Sheet		
I have to...	**Do I know how to?**	**Where I can get help...**
(List study skills you have to use below	(Yes, No, Maybe)	(From the teacher, librarian, friend, family, etc.)

Teacher's Role

When teachers are clear about how they will evaluate assignments and learnings and specify their criteria and requirements for assignments and learnings, students can use this information when they self-assess and reflect on their work. (Refer back to numbers 5 and 6 on Figures 1–1 and 1–2.) *Teachers must be sure that students have or know the criteria for the assignment and how it will be evaluated.* Anderson and Armbruster (1984) indicated that the most effective approaches to study assignments are those that are the best match to the criteria that the teacher will use to assess students' learning and performance. For example, students in Mrs. Argueta's class would *not* do very well if their approach to writing the research report on rainforests focused on summarizing their textbook chapter on the rainforest and using *only* National Geographic videos to supplement this information. Instead, because Mrs. Argueta made students aware of the criteria for the assignment and how it will be evaluated, they would do much better to focus on using library materials and the Internet to research one aspect of rainforests; specifically, Mrs. Argueta wants them to use *at least four* different library sources and at least *one* Website, including books, newspapers, magazines, encyclopedias (print or CD-ROM), and the Internet.

However, all students may not have "performance awareness." Alvermann and Phelps (2002) have indicated that performance awareness enables students to monitor whether they have understood the task and used appropriate study skills and strategies (p. 365). They have suggested that a good way to develop students' performance awareness is to ask students to determine whether the strategies they used for study or for an assignment were effective (p. 367). Teachers can use the following list, which I have created using some of Alvermann and Phelps's ideas and some of my own, to develop performance awareness with elementary through middle school students:

1. When students are finished with an assignment that involved study and learning strategies, ask them to make a list of all the strategies they used to complete the assignment. (For younger elementary children, the teacher can ask children to draw a picture of the strategies they used, or tell about the strategies they used.)

2. Ask students to tell how each strategy helped them.

3. Ask students to rate the strategies from most helpful to least helpful.

4. Ask students to share with the group which strategies were most helpful to them, telling "why" and "how."

5. The teacher can participate and share how she (or he) did the assignment, the strategies she used, and which were most helpful and why. (If the children are younger elementary students or if students do not fully understand what the teacher wants them to do, the teacher should provide a model by sharing her strategy use, and so on, before students are asked to list, rate, and discuss their study strategies.)

Students' Role

Reflection and metacognition are important to students' performance awareness. As shown, teachers can help students develop their performance awareness by asking students to reflect and consider "how they learned." Students can help themselves, too, by being reflective learners and thinkers. Figure 1–6 shows a student reflection guide developed for use with elementary to middle school students. When you first introduce this guide, it is suggested that you model the questions and answers for

Figure 1–6 Student reflection guide

Student Reflection Guide

1. Did I complete the study or learning assignments as explained by the teacher? (To be sure, compare the teacher's criteria to your work and see if it is complete or finished.)

2. What kind of grade or evaluation do I think I will get on this assignment, activity, or test? Why?

3. Is there something else I could do to get a better grade or evaluation on it? What?

4. Do I have the time to do more to get the better grade? How much more time do I need? Will it be worth it?

5. What did I learn from this study or assignment? Is this what the teacher was expecting me to learn? Is there something else I can do to learn more or to meet the teacher's criteria? Am I willing to do it? Why or why not?

6. Overall, am I satisfied with my learning or work? Why or why not? If not, how can I improve it?

your students with an assignment they have recently completed. Then, when students see how you use it, they can try it out on their own in small groups. The reflection questions can be answered orally, in written responses, or in a check-sheet type of format. The most important idea is for students to realize that they have a good bit of the control of their learning and of how well they learn and do on their assignments. Encourage them to remember to ask themselves these or similar reflection questions whenever they do a study-learning assignment.

Reflection Activity 1.2

What studying and learning considerations do you view as most important and why? Can you point out experiences with various students and the classrooms you have worked in to further support your views?

Learning How to Learn: A Summary

The focus of this chapter has been on learning how to learn. This focus crosses all subject area boundaries, just as the development of reading and writing are not limited to any one content area. In fact, teaching students how to learn may be the most critical goal a teacher can strive for. It can be achieved through teacher-directed practice, guidance, mentoring, and a clear understanding of the task at hand, as well as the skills, strategies, and tools needed to successfully complete the work. Learning how to learn is optimally a team effort between teacher and student, and both parties should be committed to achieving the end result: a student who can effectively direct his or her own learning.

Try It Out

1. Sometimes when students have learned something, they are not necessarily aware of how they acquired the information. Ask them how they know they learned, then prompt them to list as many steps of the learning process as they can recall. When students think through several of these learning processes, they can begin to see a pattern in learning strategies that have helped them in the past. This can be valuable information for future learning.

2. Many Websites on the Internet have been devised, written, and posted by children. These sites cover a wide range of topics. If you are studying rainforests, for example, find a site posted by some other class that deals with that subject. Or, check out the Website created by Mrs. Hennessy's fourth-grade class from Prince Edward Island at *www.edu.pe.ca/fortune/rain.htm*. Have your students critique the material and its presentation. Next ask them to consider the extent to which the Website creators learned as they developed their own site.

3. As an extension of the previous activity, have students check some of the factual data on the Website with cross-research to verify its accuracy. Encourage them to talk about their findings.

Teaching Strategies and Activities

Many of the good teaching strategies you already use with students to enhance various aspects of their literacy development are equally applicable to enhancing their study skills and strategies. For example, teaching strategies such as modeling, scaffolding, metacognitive questioning, cooperative learning, and peer and cross-age tutoring are very effective for developing study-learning skills and strategies. These teaching tools are really fundamental to all teaching and student learning. They are not just literacy education strategies. In fact, more and more of these strategies are being suggested, although sometimes under different names or labels, across all the elementary and middle school curriculum areas (see Hyde and Bizar 1996; Kauchak and Eggen 2003; Maxim 2003; Sivertsen 1993). In this chapter, each of these teaching strategies is highlighted, along with specific examples relative to a focus on study and learning skills/strategies. Additionally, the "scaffolded reading experience" is introduced with examples of pre-, post-, and during-reading activities in Mrs. Argueta's fourth-grade classroom to illustrate the application of many of the teaching strategies discussed in this chapter.

Modeling

Modeling is the most basic and important of teaching strategies. In fact, research indicates that teacher modeling is one of the most powerful strategies a teacher can use (Bandura 1993). Teachers use modeling throughout their curriculum by the many examples they provide students. These demonstrations and examples show students *what* the teacher expects and *how* the skill, strategy, or activity is done. Through modeling by the teacher, students are provided concrete examples and performance criteria.

Even the youngest of children benefit by the modeling of their parents or other significant caregivers. For example, when visiting our (then) seven-and-a-half-month-old granddaughter, Elena, we observed her attempting to drink from her baby cup—however, because she didn't tip it backwards, she didn't get the drink she wanted. Our son, Todd, called to his daughter across the table and "modeled" for Elena, saying, "Like this," while tipping his head back and holding a cup to his own lips. Elena immediately got the idea, and we were delighted to see her imitate her dad and successfully get her drink. Likewise, Elena has been repeatedly read to by her parents, my husband and I, and other family members and caregivers. Because of this modeling of the turning of pages, storytelling, and looking at the pictures on each page, Elena, even at seven-and-a-half-months, would pick up her favorite board books, turn the pages, and look at the pictures. By eighteen months, Elena's favorite activity was turning through each page of her books and naming the characters, colors, and things she knew best. She "read" her books at naptime, during playtime, and throughout the day's activities.

Some specific examples of the modeling teaching strategy, relative to study and learning skills, follow in the scenario that takes place in Susan Abrams's classroom. Susan is an early-grade elementary teacher. This, in fact, is only her second year of teaching second grade, but Susan is a quick study. Based on her experiences, many good, but some disastrous, with her class last school year, Susan is making a concerted, planned effort to "model" the study and learning skills/strategies she is expecting of her students, even on the first day of school.

Susan lists the items on the chalkboard that students are to bring to class tomorrow (on their second day of school). She asks the students to copy the list. While she gives them time to copy it, Susan also can be seen copying the list into her own notebook so the students know *what* she expects. She tells the children that she is writing it down so that she will have a record of every item she has asked them to bring. That way she won't forget any of it. She then puts the list in her own book bag, saying: "This is important, so I'm going to put it in my book bag so I don't lose it." The students see *how* Susan keeps important things from getting lost.

Susan gives out the new social studies book on the community and community helpers and heroes to each child. This new book will provide much of the most basic content information for the class's first unit of study this school year. Susan plans to integrate the community curriculum with reading, writing, and the other language arts, as well as with several fine arts projects she is planning for the class. But first she wants to "model" *what* she wants the students to do and *how* to find things in this new book. She knows that these children did not have any content textbooks in their first-grade classrooms last school year, so she models locating the table of contents, using the table of contents to find where various chapters begin, locating the index, and using the index to find out where the information on firefighters can be found in the book. (The first community heroes they will learn about will be firefighters.)

Following snack break, Susan reads the children the pages from their text on firefighters and also a library book about firefighters. Then she reads them excerpts from some newspaper clippings she collected about the heroism of these community helpers. Susan makes an assignment: During the next several weeks, the children, with the help of their families, are to collect their own newspaper clippings of firefighter heroism, citing the name of the newspaper; title of the news article; page number; author of the news article; and on a separate sheet of paper that the children must attach to the clipping, one or two sentences telling how the firefighters were heroes. Susan gives a demonstration for two of the clippings she read. She has modeled *what* she wants them to do and *how* she wants them to do it.

Scaffolding

Scaffolding is almost a natural extension of modeling. First we (teachers as well as family members) "model." Then we follow it up as needed, using "scaffolding." Wharton-MacDonald, Pressley, and Hampston's (1998) research indicates that effective first-grade teachers provide extensive scaffolding to help their students become self-regulatory and independent. Older elementary through middle school students benefit from scaffolding as well. In *Assessing Readers* (Flippo 2003), I provide examples of scaffolding reading instruction and explain that the scaffolding teaching strategy first involves the teacher presenting a task to the student by modeling the task. Then the teacher observes the student perform the task, noting what the student can do and what the student may be having difficulty with. Next the teacher introduces and models small modifications of the task to help the student be more successful with it. In other words, the teacher tries to scaffold from least support (just modeling alone) to most support, depending on the learner's observed needs. The teacher only provides and models additional support as needed. The idea is that when the student can do the task independently, without support, the support modifications are removed.

Think in terms of using the training wheels on a youngster's bicycle. Some youngsters need the extra support longer than others, but when the training wheel modification is no longer needed, the support should be removed for independent cycling. In the next scenario, we see how a veteran teacher, Patricia Roberts, scaffolds the study and learning skills development of her third-grade students.

This academic year, Patricia's students have a particularly wide range of study and learning skills/strategies, strengths, and needs. Patricia is particularly interested in giving the more proficient learners as much opportunity as possible to pursue independent options and work, freeing herself for spending more instructional time with the students who need it the most. It is mid-school year, and the students will be required to do more textbook assignments; they must be able to use the glossaries in their books as well as dictionaries as resources when needed. Patricia has been carefully observing how individual students manage these tasks, and she is aware of who needs scaffolded instruction to provide needed *support*. What follows is an instructional dialogue with one student, Stacy, who is inefficient at finding words in the dictionary. Patricia has observed that when Stacy is looking for a word, she turns every page in the dictionary, from front to back, in search of the particular word.

MS. ROBERTS: Stacy, when I was reading your science book assignment, I came across the word "electron." It wasn't one of the words listed in the glossary, and I wasn't sure exactly what it was, so I decided to look it up in the dictionary. Here's how I did it. (Ms. Roberts demonstrates/models and at the same time verbalizes how she finds "electron" using alphabetical order.) Do you want to find another word that begins with the letter "e" in the assigned reading in your science book and show me how you find it in the dictionary?

STACY: Okay, how about this one? It is spelled "element." (Stacy spells it out.) I will stay in the "e" part of the dictionary and watch for that word. (Stacy demonstrates as she turns through each of the "e" pages until she finds "element.")

MS. ROBERTS: That is very good: You went directly to the place where the "e" words begin before you began looking at every page. What if you used the next letter clues to find the word more quickly? (Ms. Roberts models and at the same time verbalizes how she finds "element" more quickly.) What do you think, Stacy—can you do that with another "e" word?

STACY: I think so. Let's find another "e" word in the book and I'll try it. (Stacy selects the word "experiment" and traces the steps she uses, finding it letter by letter in the dictionary.)

MS. ROBERTS: Fantastic, I think you have it. Now why don't I show you one shortcut that I know. Close the dictionary and watch how I can find "experiment" by using alphabetical order *and* the guide words at the tops of the pages as a shortcut. (Ms. Roberts models and verbalizes how the guide words can make the process even faster.)

STACY: I can do that. Can we make it harder now? Let's find a word in the science assignment that begins with another letter. (Stacy selects a word beginning with an "n" and successfully models and verbalizes how she uses the guide words to find it. Even though she is still slower than she'll be with more experience, the scaffolding has already been successful for her.)

Reflection Activity 2.1

Since we were young children, we have been learning through modeling and scaffolding. Can you recall an example of how you've learned through modeling and/or how you've helped someone else learn through scaffolding?

Metacognitive Questioning

In *Assessing Readers* (Flippo 2003), I define metacognitive awareness as an advanced cognition process that involves the learner's awareness of his or her own understanding. I further explain metacognitive questioning, or metacognitive probing, as an assessment and instructional teaching strategy that involves asking students many questions, or "probes," in order to find out more about their cognitive processes and to help students become more metacognitively aware (p. 368). Basically, the way to strengthen metacognitive awareness is to ask metacognitive questions, causing students to practice thinking about *how they know* and *justifying their responses to material they are reading and/or learning*. Therefore, metacognitive questioning is a very effective teaching strategy that can help teachers and students focus on the content being learned.

For example, if you had read and studied material on cognitive-processing theories, following your study I could question your comprehension and ask, "What have you gleaned from these theories?" However, if as a follow-up, I probed further and metacognitively questioned you by asking that you justify or explain your answer, then I would be the catalyst for your going back to the material and finding evidence to support your response. In the scenario that follows, Adam Barg, a fourth-grade teacher, uses metacognitive questioning with one of his students in order to facilitate more of a focus on the facts and details in the social studies text assignment.

MR. BARG: OK, Max—that was a good answer. I asked you to summarize the early westward movement in the United States, and you explained that farmers moved their families, farm animals, and possessions across the country. Now can you elaborate further by telling or reading to me the details of this movement?

MAX: Sure. Here in our textbook it says that the farmers had to make decisions about what they would need along the way and what they would need when they settled on their new farmland.

MR. BARG: Good; can you point out some of the specific examples given in the text and explain how those would have been especially important?

MAX: (Explains.)

MR. BARG: Very thoughtful, Max. Now what about the difficulties these people faced? Can you point those out and explain them? Be sure to use the facts in the textbook as you discuss each.

Cooperative Learning

Cooperative learning groups are defined in Flippo (2003) as students working together in a group small enough that everyone can participate in a task or project that has been clearly assigned (p. 365). Cooperative learning is a teaching tool that is planned and orchestrated by the teacher, but once the group and learning assignment or project have been explained, the teacher phases out and the students are expected to complete the assignment without the teacher's direct and immediate supervision. Slavin's (1995) work indicates that, generally, the most effective characteristics of cooperative learning include clear group goals, individual accountability, and equal opportunities for success. In Flippo (2003), I put together a listing of recommendations for organizing and managing cooperative learning groups with elementary through middle school students (pp. 219–20). Here I have summarized from that and delineated the recommendations most applicable to assignments for studying and learning from text.

- Keep the size of the groups small, with no more than four or five students per group.
- Group students with their interests and motivations in mind, but strive for heterogeneously mixed groups with regard to academic achievement and sociocultural considerations.
- Be clear concerning the learning goals and study-learning tasks that are to be accomplished.
- Set reasonable time limits for accomplishing the assignment.
- Provide initial guidance and remain available for mentoring, but do allow students to make decisions regarding the distribution of their work, leadership decisions, and other decisions as they progress with the assignment.

The scenario that follows illustrates how Ms. Chou, a fifth-grade teacher, uses cooperative learning as a teaching, learning, and organizational tool in her classroom. During the first twelve-week report card period, Ms. Chou's class will be studying Western European countries and cultures and their influence on the development of the United States and American culture from the 1600s through the present. Because there are so many possible European countries and cultures to select from, Ms. Chou decides to utilize cooperative learning groups—each one focusing on the influences and contributions of one Western European country and its various cultures. Based on self-identified student interests, the class is divided into eight small learning groups. These groups include a focus on Great Britain, Ireland, Italy, Germany, France, Spain, Portugal, and Norway. Although many countries and cultures in Western Europe will not be covered, Ms. Chou feels confident that the learning goals of her assignment will be accomplished, and because students suggested and self-selected the countries they will focus on, their motivation has been very high.

Ms. Chou delineates this research assignment as follows:

1. Using print, electronic, and multimedia sources, learn about the history of the country as it relates to reasons for emigration to North America and later to the United States.

2. Learn about the cultures that emigrated and what each contributed to the development of cultures in North America and later to the United States.

3. Document all sources and develop a bibliography of all sources used for your assignment.

4. Be prepared to present your learnings of numbers 1 and 2 to the entire class. You may plan a multimedia presentation and/or use art, drama, puppetry, graphs, written summaries, food, clothing, artifacts, and pictures to share your information.

5. You will have nine weeks to gather and prepare your information.

6. Each group will be given an entire school day during the tenth or eleventh week of this grading period to share their information with the rest of the class.

7. Each group will be evaluated on their work and to what extent their work met the learning goals and assignment tasks that have been explained and are listed in the above information.

8. Each member of the group will be evaluated by the other group members and the teacher on their work and their contribution to their group's meeting of the assigned learning goals and assignment tasks.

If these cooperative learning plans are successful, Ms. Chou hopes to use similar assignments for future grading periods in order to eventually study the Eastern European and Asian influences and contributions, as well as African, South and Central American, and Middle Eastern ones, to the development of the United States and its cultures from 1600 through the present. She is optimistic, but also realizes that she may have to vary her cooperative learning assignments or use other teaching strategies in order to hold the interests of the students.

Peer and Cross-Age Tutoring

Arthur Mahnkopf, the sixth-grade teacher across the hall, uses both peer and cross-age tutoring strategies for many of his study and learning assignments. Peer tutoring involves students helping other students of approximately the same age, in the same classroom, with their work and assignments. Cross-age tutoring involves students helping younger students with their work and assignments. The thinking is that the students being helped benefit from the extra help and attention, *and* the students doing the tutoring (the tutors) benefit because they have to know and/or learn the material first in order to help someone else with it. A review of the research supports this thinking (Taylor 2002).

Mr. Mahnkopf often pairs students in his classroom together, one very skilled in a task or area of study and the other needing extra help, in order to complete a more challenging study-learning assignment. He also has recently teamed up with Mrs. Cantrel, a first grade teacher, in a very successful cross-age tutoring endeavor. Mr. Mahnkopf's students have been going with him into Mrs. Cantrel's classroom, two or three times per week, for forty-five minutes each time. Individual sixth graders are "buddies" to the first graders, helping them with learning projects that Mrs. Cantrel has developed for the first graders to do. For example, one week they were to make and label a collage of all the things they had learned about nutrition. They were also to write sentences to list the facts that were represented by their contributions to the collage and put them in a large nutrition book they were developing. The first graders had gathered many magazine pictures to use for their collage contributions, but they needed the help of their older buddies to help spell the words for their labels. They also needed the buddies to verify and write the nutritional facts in sentences for their nutrition book as the first graders dictated them. Before each fact was written, the first grader was to show their buddy the source of the fact in their health texts in order to show their comprehension of the material they learned.

Often, the use of peer and cross-age learning groups nicely supplements and complements the use of cooperative learning groups. Although each type of learning group is different, in particular situations and with particular students' study-learning goals and needs, one might be a more effective teaching and learning strategy than the other. For example, Ms. Chou may later decide to use peer and cross-age learning arrangements as an alternative to only using cooperative learning groups in her classroom. The variation should serve more purposes and needs, and it should help keep students interested and motivated.

Reflection Activity 2.2

How would you explain to a parent or new teacher that cooperative learning groups and peer and cross-age tutoring can help students improve their study-learning skills? Could there be any drawbacks to such arrangements? How can teachers minimize these drawbacks? Could you suggest an example of an assignment in which cooperative learning and/or tutoring could be used most effectively?

Scaffolded Reading Experiences

Graves and Graves (2003) describe a "scaffolded reading experience" as a set of prereading, during-reading, and postreading activities especially designed to assist a particular group of students in successfully understanding, learning from, and enjoying a particular textual selection (p. 9). They indicate that this flexible teaching strategy was developed from research and ideas that include but are not limited to:

- the need for student success (e.g., Brophy 1986, Guthrie and Wigfield 2000)
- schema theory (Rumelhart 1980)
- constructivist ideas, including learners constructing their own meanings
- the importance of working with others, as in cooperative learning (Slavin 1987)
- interactive model ideas, especially the idea that readers use both text and their background knowledge to understand their readings
- scaffolding, which involves teacher support and a gradual release of that support as learners can take over more and more of the task demands on their own—scaffolding involves modeling, guided supported practice, and adjustment of supports, as needed

The scaffolded reading experience is a teaching strategy that can be especially appropriate to study-learning assignments and development, and it makes use of many of the teaching strategies already highlighted in this chapter. Outlined next are descriptions of the prereading, during-reading, and postreading activities that can be included in a scaffolded reading experience, taken from the extensive work of Graves and Graves (2003). Additionally, examples of how Mrs. Argueta might have implemented these activities with her study-learning assignment are provided. For a full range of additional examples, consult the Graves and Graves (2003) book *Scaffolding Reading Experiences: Designs for Student Success.*

Prereading Activities

These activities can include such things as motivating students, relating the material to students' lives, activating students' background knowledge, building their text-specific knowledge, preteaching vocabulary and other concepts, prequestioning techniques, predicting from the text, setting directions, and suggesting strategies that could work for the reading assignment.

Overall, prereading activities are intended to motivate and prepare students to read the text assignment. Any combination of prereading activities can be used. The teacher is in the best position to select and design activities appropriate to the particular students, particular assignment, and the particular reading involved. Here is an example of how Mrs. Argueta might have motivated and prepared her fourth graders for reading a text chapter selection on rainforests. Keep in mind, this is only one set of possibilities for prereading activities that Mrs. Argueta might have selected and designed:

1. Mrs. Argueta first read students a recent newspaper article she found that described how rainforests are disappearing off the face of the earth, and how their gradual disappearance is causing many kinds of animals, reptiles, insects, and plants to have no place to live.

2. Students were asked to predict what would happen to these animals, reptiles, insects, and plants.

3. Students were asked to predict what would happen to them (the students) and their families if our world, the environment in which we live, were to disappear.

4. Mrs. Argueta indicated that "the chapter that we are going to read will help us understand more about rainforests and the problems being caused by their gradual disappearance." She suggested that "as we read, individual students may want to make a list of these problems, and, later, the group will discuss them and other information about rainforests that students are interested in talking about."

During-Reading Activities

These activities can include such things as students reading silently, teacher reading to students, teacher-guided reading, students reading orally, and modifying the text. Overall, the purpose here is to have students read and interact with text so that they can construct meaning from the text. One combination of activities Mrs. Argueta could have used with her students as they read the rainforest chapter follows. Keep in mind that another teacher might have just as effectively designed different during-reading activities for a different group of students. Graves and Graves (2003, p. 110) point out some questions teachers can ask themselves to help plan this stage of activities: How might this reading task and assignment best be accomplished? What can I do to involve students actively with this text or to make this material come alive for them? What can I ask students to do as they read the text to make it more understandable, enjoyable, or memorable?

Here is what Mrs. Argueta decided:

1. She began by reading the first half of the chapter to the students herself to more fully hold their attention.

2. She modified the text by skipping several sections in the beginning and middle of the chapter that might be boring to some of the students, and she explained to them that later, if some of them were particularly interested in learning about this information, as background for their research reports, they could come back to it. In this way, she focused the reading on the parts of the chapter she thought they would find most interesting.

3. She asked them to silently read the ending of the chapter to themselves. She thought that the ending of the chapter, which described the plight of the wildlife of the rainforest, would be of particular interest to the students. She reminded students to keep taking notes about the problems they were reading about so that they could discuss them later.

Postreading Activities

These can include questioning, discussion, writing, drama, graphic, application, multimedia, and reteaching activities. Overall, these activities are intended to encourage students to do something with material they have just read. Graves and Graves (2003) suggest that "until we do something with what we have read, until we take the effort to work with the meaning we have gleaned from the text and internalize it," it isn't really ours (p. 150). Once again, the teacher must decide what activities, if any, are appropriate to any particular reading or assignment. See how Mrs. Argueta planned some postreading activities for her students to fit their assignment:

1. Students discussed the problems, which they had individually noted, that are being caused by the disappearance of rainforests. Some of these problems were of particular interest to individuals and to groups of students.

2. Mrs. Argueta used the discussion as an opportunity to reteach or highlight the important problems and associated concepts from the chapter on the chalkboard.

3. Mrs. Argueta suggested that because different students seemed particularly interested in different topics, problems, or aspects of what they read, it might be interesting to individually do research and find out more. Then students could share their research with the whole group. Mrs. Argueta assigned the research report as an application, outreach, and reading-writing activity assignment. (Refer back to Figure 1–2 for the details of Mrs. Argueta's assignment.)

4. As a follow-up to students' publishing and sharing of their research reports, Mrs. Argueta suggested and encouraged interested students to use the Internet and then email to locate and make contact with individuals and groups who are working to save the world's rainforests (e.g., send an email message to a rainforest conservation group). Students could ask questions seeking more information regarding the most current problems and aspects of the situation in which they are most interested. Students could share the reply with their classmates.

5. To continue to keep their interest active and to further motivate the students, Mrs. Argueta suggested that the class do a whole wall mural depicting the different problems and aspects of the overall

rainforest situation, based on the textbook reading, the newspaper article Mrs. Argueta read, and their individual library and Internet research, email communications, and discussion thus far. Students worked in small groups to illustrate whatever problems/aspects they were most concerned about. Students individually decided which problem-group in which to work on the mural.

Reflection Activity 2.3

Consider the benefits and examples of prereading, during-reading, and postreading activities suggested in this chapter. Which have you successfully used with students and how can they be done most effectively as part of classroom learning assignments? What "teaching tips" could you offer other teachers?

Teaching Strategies and Activities: A Summary

So much of what children, and even older students, learn is developed by observing and modeling the actions of others: parents, siblings, other family members, peers, and teachers. It is not enough to tell students what to do. They often need to be *shown* how to perform the needed skill, strategy, or task. This chapter has provided examples of modeling and scaffolding—basic teaching strategies applicable to all parts of the curriculum. Other generic, yet fundamental, teaching strategies and activities have also been explained and sampled. These include use of metacognitive questioning, cooperative learning, peer and cross-age tutoring, and scaffolded reading experiences. These strategies provide the support that students of all ages often need to learn and to develop the confidence that leads to independence and self-sufficiency as learners.

1. Scaffolding is a natural extension of modeling; therefore, teachers often follow up modeling with scaffolding support. On your next assignment, model for your students how to get started on the assignment, especially what you want them to do and how you want them to do it. Then allow your students to begin, watching for any individuals who are struggling with the task. If any of your students are struggling with getting started, take them aside and give them more assistance and support. For example, if students are doing a research assignment, work with the students to locate the first resource. Then step aside again and observe the students to determine their progress. Continue to scaffold support as needed based on your ongoing observations of individual students.

2. Metacognitive questioning takes time, and teachers are already pressed for time to accomplish all of the tasks, activities, and teaching that must be crammed into each school day. As an experiment to ascertain whether the additional time is *really* worth it, try it out over a few weeks with some students. See if the metacognitive questioning provides you with more insight into individual student's comprehension of the material. See if the questioning helps students focus more on the content that is being read and learned.

3. If your students are interested in developing and posting to their own Website as a postreading activity, for example, as part of the rainforest research assignment Mrs. Argueta has given her class, suggest that they review other Websites on rainforests for ideas, and then using their own research information (electronic and nonelectronic), develop their own site. Ask students to later share the Website with the class and explain *how they decided what to include and what not to include on the Website(s).*

4. Interested students could prepare their postreading research reports as a slide show in Microsoft PowerPoint to share with their class or with other classes. Students should be encouraged to explain *how they decided what were the most important points to include and why.*

Use of Teacher-Developed Study Guides

Study guides are another set of effective teaching tools for developing and enhancing the study-learning skills and strategies of students. Because there are so many types of study guides available, I have devoted this entire chapter to them and developed an example to illustrate each of them that I have found particularly useful for elementary through middle school grades. It should be noted that *the purpose of the study guides is to help students learn the material in the text, not to just focus on reading, writing, or researching*—some of these classic study guides use reading, some use reading and writing, some involve reading, research, and writing, and so on. Additionally, the examples have been developed with expository text, rather than narratives. Expository text (content materials) typically involve a focus on information-type reading, making it the more appropriate material to use with study guides.

Wood, Lapp, and Flood (1992) provide an extensive and comprehensive review of study guides, including the many different types of study guides, and how to use them. They explain that study guides are teacher-developed tools for helping students understand instructional reading materials. These guides often consist of a series of activities or questions related to the text or other materials students will use in class or for study. Students engage in the activities or respond to the questions as they read and pursue their assignments (p. 1).

Using study guides with reading assignments gives teachers some control over the concepts and ideas they hope students will learn, and it provides students with a clear understanding of what the teacher expects them to know. Furthermore, study guides provide support and assistance to students, without taking all control away from them. Students use the study guide, thereby retaining some control of their own learning (Wood et al. 1992).

Classroom teachers can use numerous types of study guides to direct students' reading and learning. Wood, Lapp, and Flood (1992) have emphasized that these study guides should be used carefully and that the teacher should always remember that they are only to be used as a stepping-stone to independent learning. Once students have a successful strategy for learning from the text, the study guide should be obsolete. Teachers' ultimate purpose is to lead students to the point where they can independently read and study on their own without the support of a study guide (p. 4). Although Wood, Lapp, and Flood (1992) described many different types of study guides, I have selected only those that are appropriate for use with primary grade and intermediate grade elementary-age students as well as with middle school students and also are most appropriate for use as a study-learning tool. See Figure 3–1 for my overview of these selected study guides, which was developed by summarizing descriptions provided by Wood, Lapp, and Flood (1992); then see the sections that follow for more information and an example of each. Additionally, I recommend that interested readers also refer to Wood, Lapp, and Flood (1992) and other references cited in this chapter for more descriptions and examples of these as well as other study guides.

Point-of-View Guide

In the Point-of-View Guide (Wood 1988), students are asked questions in an interview-type format to help them gain different perspectives on

Overview of Study Guides

Type of study guide	For study-learning materials in:	Use/purpose of study guide:
Point-of-view guide	• History • Science	• To help students elaborate as they read • To help students develop mental recitation skills • To help students learn content
Interactive reading guide	• Social Studies • Science • Other content area learning	• To promote cooperative reading and learning • To promote use of predictions, associations, and recalling and reorganizing information
Extended anticipation guide	• Literature • All content area learning	• To stimulate thinking and activate prior knowledge • To stimulate hypothesizing and discussion
Concept guide	• All content area learning	• To help students organize and categorize subordinate information under major concepts
Analogical study guide	• Science • Other content area learning	• To help students make abstract concepts more understandable • To encourage students to connect new information with their everyday experiences
Reading road map	• All content area learning	• To help guide students through reading materials by helping them adjust their reading rate to correspond with the importance of the information they encounter
Glossing	• Literature • All content area learning	• To help direct students' attention as they read, improving their understanding of the text • To use marginal notes in the text to help engage students as they read/study

Developed and adapted from information in Karen D. Wood, Diane Lapp, and James Flood (1992). *Guiding Readers Through Text: A Review of Study Guides.* Newark, DE: International Reading Association.

the events or information described in the reading materials. Teachers should usually model the kinds of responses they hope to solicit from students when they begin. See the following questions that have been developed to go with encyclopedia articles on the "Pilgrims," "Mayflower," "Mayflower Compact," and "William Bradford." Keep in mind that similar kinds of questions could be developed for use with content textbook materials, magazine articles, and other study-learning materials.

"Pilgrims" (Volume 15, pp. 415–16)

1. As one of the pilgrims, tell why you came to America.

2. Explain what led up to your coming to America and who your leaders were.

"Mayflower" (Volume 13, p. 261)

3. What was the name of the ship that you came on and what was the trip like?

"Mayflower Compact" (Volume 13, pp. 261–62)

4. You were one of the signers of the Mayflower Compact. Tell us what it was and what it was for.

"William Bradford" (Volume 2, p. 454)

5. William Bradford was a friend of yours. Tell about him and what he did for the colonists.

Interactive Reading Guide

The Interactive Reading Guide (Wood 1988) is a study guide that promotes cooperative learning. The teacher directs the use of the guide by asking for responses from individuals, small groups, pairs of students, or from the whole class by use of symbols. When students complete each part, activity, or question, the teacher instigates a class discussion of the material. This is a good technique to use when the teacher feels that the entire class needs additional help or guidance with a particular reading and study assignment. See the questions and symbols detailed in Figure 3–2 for an example of how a teacher might develop an Interactive Reading Guide for a social studies selection and study on the students' state. These third-grade students live in Massachusetts.

Figure 3–2   Massachusetts: A study guide for group interaction

Massachusetts

Directions: Use the interaction codes to tell you who to work with. Then read the directions for each one and do what it says. If you need help, ask someone in your group or the teacher.

Interaction codes:
- ○ = Work alone
- ⊛ = Work with your group
- ∞ = Work with a partner
- ◯ = The whole class will work on this together

⊛ 1. In your group, list everything you can think of that you know about Massachusetts.

○
∞ 2. On your own, or with a partner, read pages 59–60 and see if you can write down anything else you found out about Massachusetts.

⊛ 3. Share the new things you found out in your group, and add all the new things to the group list.

◯ 4. The whole class will share their lists and one big class list will be made. We will all look at the map of Massachusetts to see if anything we listed happens in any particular places.

Developed and adapted from the creative ideas and an example in Karen D. Wood (1988), " Guiding Students Through Informational Text," *The Reading Teacher, 41*(9), pp. 912–20.

Extended Anticipation Guide

Duffelmeyer, Baum, and Merkley (1987) developed the idea of the Extended Anticipation Guide, which stimulates discussion, provides opportunities for the teacher to find out what students know about a topic, and stimulates prior knowledge and hypothesizing. Duffelmeyer (1994) further recommended the anticipation guide, which evolved from Herber's (1978) ideas, as a prereading teaching strategy; Duffelmeyer also indicated that the guide can be used to promote reading to learn from expository text. See Figure 3–3 for an example of what an Extended Anticipation Guide for the study of "bats" might look like. This one was developed for use in a second-grade classroom.

Concept Guide

Baker (1977) originated Concept Guides to help students see the relationship of more- and less-significant concepts. These guides are designed to help students organize information from texts, categorizing information and listing subordinate information under major concepts. This is similar to the process students must use when they outline information, and it can serve as an important text-study technique. See Figure 3–4 for one sample of a Concept Guide. This one was developed for fifth graders for their readings on and study of jellyfish, which was part of their marine science unit.

Analogical Study Guide

Bean, Singer, and Cowan (1985) developed the Analogical Study Guide to reinforce learning of content area materials. Use of these guides encourages students to connect new information with known information, and

Figure 3–3 Extended anticipation guide for the study of bats

Bats

Directions: Read the sentences in Part I. If you agree, put a ☺ in the column. If you disagree, put a ☹ in the column. Be ready to explain your choices.

Part I

Agree   Disagree

_____   _____   1. Bats are only in scary movies and Halloween stories.

_____   _____   2. Bats live in dark, wet places.

_____   _____   3. Bats are a kind of bird.

_____   _____   4. Bats have very bad eyesight.

Directions: Read about bats in your "Weekly Reader." If you read something that supports your choices, put a ☺ in the column. If what you read doesn't support your choices, put a ☹ in the column. Then write what the "Weekly Reader" says about bats, using your own words.

Part II

Support   No support   In your own words

1. _____   _____   _____
                          _____

2. _____   _____   _____
                          _____

3. _____   _____   _____
                          _____

4. _____   _____   _____
                          _____

Developed and adapted from the creative ideas and an example in F. A. Duffelmeyer, D. D. Baum, and D. J. Merkley (1987), "Maximizing Reader-Text Confrontation with an Extended Anticipation Guide," *Journal of Reading, 31*, pp. 146–50.

Figure 3–4   Concept guide on jellyfish

Jellyfish

Part I

Directions: Read each of the statements given below. If you believe them to be true, check the "true" column. If you believe them to be false, check the "false" column.

True	False	**Information statements**
_____	_____	1. Jellyfish are sea animals.
_____	_____	2. Jellyfish get their names from the jellylike material between two layers of cells that make up the animal's body.
_____	_____	3. The jellyfish body looks like a bell or umbrella shape.
_____	_____	4. A group of projections, called tentacles, hang down from the body.
_____	_____	5. Corals, sea anemones, and hydras are also sea animals.
_____	_____	6. Some jellyfish can inflict painful and sometimes poisonous stings into people and other animals.
_____	_____	7. Sea wasps are a kind of jellyfish.
_____	_____	8. Sea nettles are a kind of jellyfish.

Part II

Directions: Read the information given in your textbook, in the encyclopedia article, and in the *National Geographic* article on jellyfish. Then organize each of the informational statements given above, in Part I, under one of the following three headings. If you find other information that you think should go under a heading, go ahead and list it and we can discuss these in class.

Headings

"Kinds of Sea Animals"

_____

_____

_____

       "Types of Jellyfish"

         _____

         _____

         _____

                "Characteristics of Jellyfish"

                  _____

                  _____

                  _____

Developed and adapted from the creative ideas and an example in Karen D. Wood, Diane Lapp, and James Flood (1992). *Guiding Readers Through Text: A Review of Study Guides,* p. 52. Newark, DE: International Reading Association.

helps make abstract ideas more understandable. Bean, Singer, and Cowan suggested three steps in developing these guides:

1. Analyze the reading-learning task to determine what concepts students should learn, focusing on the most essential information.

2. Construct appropriate analogies for the material to be learned.

3. Explain and demonstrate to the students how the guide works, showing how analogies are used as retrieval/memory cues (mnemonic devices) to help students recall and remember information from the text material to be learned.

Wood, Lapp, and Flood (1992) suggested that by using small, cooperative groups, teachers can encourage students to brainstorm and come up with their own analogies for the material to be learned. Furthermore, teachers can creatively use known information to help students learn more difficult material. Here is an example of some analogies developed in a Wood, Lapp, and Flood example of how a primary-grade teacher used an Analogical Study Guide to help students see how a plant receives nutrients by drinking water in similar ways to a person drinking through a straw. After students read a selection with the teacher, the teacher provided a poster identifying plant parts and their functions, and then showed a second poster of a person drinking through a straw. The study guide contained some of these analogies:

1. root to cup (collects and holds nutrients/food/water)

2. stem to straw (carries food/water/nutrients upward)

3. leaf to person drinking (receives food/water/nutrients)

Reading Road Map

Wood, Lapp, and Flood (1992) explained that the Reading Road Map (Wood 1988) helps guide students through the reading and study of text that otherwise might be particularly difficult for students who have not yet learned to adjust their reading rate. They have indicated that it is particularly important to explain the purpose of the Reading Road Map to the students and suggested that parallels can be drawn between the textbook journey and an actual trip to another location. Figure 3–5 illustrates an example of a Reading Road Map, stimulated from the creative ideas and an example provided in Wood (1988), to help you see how a teacher can use this to guide students through the readings for a unit of study.

Glossing

Otto et al. (1981) are credited with demonstrating how the use of marginal notes, or glossing, can help students understand textual reading materials. Glossing can be used to direct students' attention to specific content of the reading by pointing out facts, information, and important concepts in the piece. This technique involves the teacher writing in the margins of the material. Because of this, teachers may choose to use an overhead projector to point out and highlight the material. The kind of notations that teachers choose to make will depend on the age and needs of the students, and the content to be focused on and learned. Wood, Lapp, and Flood (1992) suggested that teachers make sure that the gloss notations are brief and used only to meet lesson objectives. Teachers will not want the notations to make the reading more cumbersome and difficult for students. I developed a short example of a teacher's glossing of material on spiders to illustrate what this may look like (see Figure 3–6). You also can let students gloss their own reading and study material to highlight and note information they believe is important or helpful for them to learn. See Figure 3–7 for an example of how a student glossed this same material.

Figure 3–5 Reading road map for the study of spiders

Reading Road Map: Spiders

Directions: Our science unit on spiders will uncover a lot of new and interesting information. Some of the information in our textbook, other books on spiders, and in our *National Geographic* articles will have to be found and read more carefully in order to not miss important information and details. To make this more of an adventure for you, we will go on a "trip" through two of the materials we will be reading using this Road Map for Spiders. The map will point out important places to slow down, and think and write about what you are learning. The map will also point out places you can read more quickly and other road map clues and signs for speed.

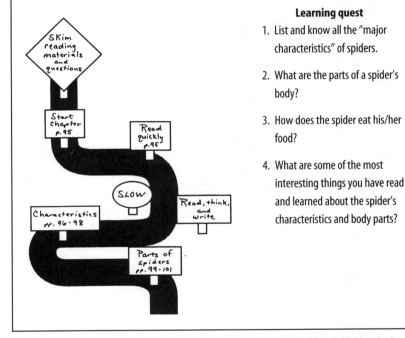

Learning quest

1. List and know all the "major characteristics" of spiders.

2. What are the parts of a spider's body?

3. How does the spider eat his/her food?

4. What are some of the most interesting things you have read and learned about the spider's characteristics and body parts?

Developed and adapted from the creative ideas and an example in Karen D. Wood (1988), "Guiding Students Through Informational Text," *The Reading Teacher, 41*(9), pp. 912–20.

(continues)

Figure 3–5   Reading road map for the study of spiders (*continued*)

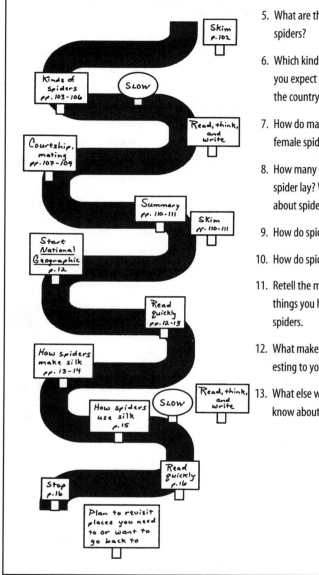

5. What are the different kinds of spiders?

6. Which kinds of spiders would you expect to find in our part of the country? Why?

7. How do male spiders attract female spiders?

8. How many eggs can a female spider lay? What is the most fun about spiderlings?

9. How do spiders weave silk?

10. How do spiders use silk?

11. Retell the most interesting things you have learned about spiders.

12. What makes these most interesting to you?

13. What else would you like to know about spiders?

Figure 3–6　Sample of teacher's glossing of material on spiders

Spiders

The spider is a small, [eight-legged] animal. Spiders are best known for the [spinning of silk] webs, which they use [to catch insects to eat.] The webs are so strong that even large insects have trouble escaping from (the spider's web.) Even though all spiders spin silk, they do not all make webs. Some spiders use the silk to trap other insects in different ways. For example, the bolas spider spins a single line of silk that is sticky at the end. The bolas spider (swings the line at insects) that fly near and catch them at the end of the line. [In this chapter, much more interesting information on spiders will be described and discussed.]

What are two characteristics of spiders?

How do spiders use silk to catch insects?

This is one way spiders use silk to catch insects.

This is another way.

What do you think this chapter will be about?

Developed and adapted from the creative ideas and an example in Karen D. Wood, Diane Lapp, and James Flood (1992). *Guiding Readers Through Text: A Review of Study Guides,* p. 65. Newark, DE: International Reading Association.

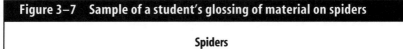

Figure 3–7   Sample of a student's glossing of material on spiders

Spiders

[The spider is a small, eight-legged animal.] Spiders are[best known for the spinning of silk webs,]which they use to catch insects to eat. The webs are so strong that even large insects have trouble escaping from the spider's web. [Even though all spiders spin silk, they do not all make webs.] Some spiders use the silk to trap other insects in different ways. For example,[the bolas spider spins a single line of silk that is sticky at the end.] The bolas spider swings the line at insects that fly near and catch them at the end of the line. In this chapter, much more interesting information on spiders will be described and discussed.

Spiders have 8 legs

Spiders spin silk

Not all spiders make webs! (This looks important to remember!)

The Bolas Spider is one kind of spider.

Use of Teacher-Developed Study Guides: A Summary

In *Becoming a Nation of Readers* (Anderson et al. 1985), the authors indicate that it is a teacher's job to instruct students in strategies for extracting and organizing important information from their texts (p. 71). The study guides and the glossing procedures sampled in this chapter were developed for just that purpose: to help students find information, organize the information, and learn from this material in their expository texts. When reading expository text, knowing what to look for before and during reading, and knowing how to manage the facts and other information gleaned during and after reading, can be crucial to students' learning and achievement. Teachers should, of course, select study guides that are most appropriate to the text, the information to be learned, and their students' needs. The goal is to provide students support in learning from text until they begin developing their own strategies for reading and learning from expository materials.

Try It Out

1. After trying out the various study guides sampled in this chapter, ask your students to determine which study guides or aids have been most effective for their individual learning of content materials. This information will help you plan for the future use of these guides. It will also enable your students to take a more active part in making decisions about their own learning.

2. Development of study guides for specific content material and text readings is *time-consuming*. However, the development of the guides is also an invaluable learning opportunity. For instance, in order to develop the guides for this chapter, I had to *really learn* the content of the material I developed each one for. Why not ask your students to develop study guides? Each week or every other week, a different group of students can be responsible for developing a guide (their choice of guides) to go with the next social studies or science chapter. The developers will have maximum opportunity to learn the material as they develop the guide, plus the rest of the class will enjoy and should benefit by use of the student-developed guide.

Study-Learning Skills and Strategies

What are the study-learning skills that elementary through middle school students must develop and learn how to use? After reviewing the literature and research for the development of study and learning skills (e.g., Caverly, Orlando, and Mullen 2000; Flippo, Becker, and Wark 2000), I have grouped the study-learning skills into three categories: reference and research skills, organizational skills, and specialized study-learning skills. Each of these categories of study-learning skills is discussed in this chapter in the sections that follow, with definitions and examples for your reference.

Reference and Research Skills

Reference and research skills are used to locate information from a variety of sources (e.g., library materials and reference sources, including encyclopedias—both print and nonprint—and the Internet), to use the dictionary, and to gather information on an infinite variety of topics (either teacher-directed, self-directed, or both). Elementary school students should be encouraged to develop these skills as early as possible because they will use them extensively in content-reading assignments as well as in personal-interest research areas as they continue to move up through the grades. Armbruster and Armstrong (1993) indicated that students in elementary school are expected to engage in search tasks ranging from locating a single fact for answering a question to locating and synthesizing information for a report. For example, a primary-grade teacher may ask students to use trade books and supplementary materials, in addition to their textbooks, to locate information about a particular topic. As students reach the upper elementary grades and beyond, the need to use these research skills and others is further intensified. Thus, the development and refinement of these skills is important if students are to succeed in doing content-related research assignments or to locate specific information of their own choosing.

A study with fifth graders searching for information in a textbook (Dreher and Sammons 1994) confirmed an earlier study (Cole and Gardner 1979) that students need guidance and real context to convert their verbal understandings to actual competence. Search tasks are common school and workplace demands (Dreher 1993). Search tasks involve a type of strategic reading that occurs when readers seek specific goal-related or assignment-related information. The task often involves looking for very specific information and ignoring irrelevant or non-task-specific information. Research has indicated (see Dreher and Sammons 1994) that search-strategy instruction using real social studies and other school subjects' research projects should improve the likelihood of the transfer of search-related skills to students. Salend (2001), in his text directed toward creating inclusive classrooms, suggested a similar need for authenticity and using real classroom textbooks for the study and learning assignments for all students. Just telling students how to research and/or teaching reference and research skills in isolation from real research and text assignments is not effective.

Miller (1979) has identified some of the more widely used library skills that should be developed in the primary grades. Other educators (cf. Nelson 1973) have also suggested that closer cooperation between the school librarian and teacher is essential if students are to effectively learn how to use reference and research skills, and that close cooperation between schools and public libraries would also be beneficial in helping reinforce student use of these study skills (McCabe 1984). Finally, in their comprehensive review of various library and research skills of college students, Allgood et al. (2000) indicated that there is a difference between library skills (which involve searching for information) and research skills (which involve searching for knowledge) (p. 204); they also implied that all students need relevant assignments to use these skills, not workbook-type practice exercises that have little to do with what is required of students in their subject areas.

Reference and research skills that can be developed and cultivated with the teacher's guidance and modeling include the use of the dictionary, encyclopedias (print or electronic), use of Internet facilities such as search engines for research, and other reference materials and the use of the library card catalog or computerized catalog to find additional sources. Using the dictionary involves knowing how to alphabetize and use guide words to locate specific words and knowing the meaning of words to further one's search purposes. Also, the ability to find and comprehend information about a particular topic in reference materials is helpful for a better understanding of many content texts and assignments. Therefore, your students' abilities to use reference materials in the library, encyclopedias, and other printed materials, as well as electronic sources, should be encouraged and developed as early as possible in the elementary classroom. Likewise, the ability to use the different types of library card catalogs (and in many school districts and public libraries, a computerized version of this) is important if your students are to locate and use information in the library. Furthermore, the use of these resources requires that students really know the topic or subject being sought and are able to generate other descriptors for the topic in the event it is listed in other ways.

Elementary teachers, even of the primary and intermediate grades, can develop many relevant reference and research learning assignments for their students. These assignments can easily fit the curriculum for the various content area units and integrated units that they teach. Refer back to Mrs. Argueta's assignment, earlier in this book, for an idea of how this can be done. It is not hard to be authentic when you believe in and teach an authentic curriculum. What ideas for authentic reference and research assignments have you developed or would you develop for the students and the curriculum in your classroom?

Reflection Activity 4.1

What are some ideas you could suggest for developing a reference and research skills assignment for elementary and/or middle school youngsters that leads them to use library books and resources, encyclopedias, dictionaries, and other reference materials (print and electronic) to locate and learn specific information? How can teachers make the assignment real, motivating, and part of the authentic learning of the content?

Organizational Skills

These skills require an ability to synthesize and evaluate material so that it can be organized into an efficient learning format. Because higher-level cognitive functions are used in organizational activities, it is important that students become more aware of their responsibility in self-initiating and self-regulating their own reading and learning behaviors (Tierney 1982). Metacognitive behavior, which involves self-awareness, self-monitoring, and self-control while learning, should be cultivated and used as part of developing necessary organizational study-learning skills. The research and literature has indicated that teachers and learners need to do more than be aware; they must further develop their awareness and knowledge to make teaching and learning more effective. This is particularly true if students are to cultivate their analysis, synthesis, and judgment among other higher-order thinking skills (see Baker and Brown 1984; Bereiter and Scardamalia 1987; Dansereau 1985; Dreher and Slater 1992; Mier 1984; Palincsar and

Brown 1984; Paris, Wasik, and Tuner 1991; Pearson and Fielding 1991; Roehler and Duffy 1991).

The organizational skills included and detailed in this section are the study-learning skills of outlining, which involves classifying, summarizing, and sequencing information; underlining and student glossing, which involves selecting or noting important information in texts; and note taking and note making, which again involves classifying, summarizing, and sequencing information.

Outlining

The primary objective of outlining is to locate and list the main ideas and supporting details in a selection. By doing this, students are better able to identify and learn the information that is important for them to read and understand. Harris and Sipay (1990, p. 617) suggested the following procedure to teach students the effective use of outlining:

1. Discuss the importance of outlining with your students.

2. Demonstrate how to outline using previously read material.

3. Present a series of exercises in outlining in which a lot of assistance to the students is given at first, and then less and less assistance is provided.

In the first step of outlining instruction, the teacher discusses the importance of each idea, its relationship to other ideas in the selection, and its place in the selection. The demonstration step involves you outlining a selection that your students are familiar with, and then modeling for them how and why certain ideas are outlined as they are. The last step of this procedure involves several substeps. These substeps include (a) displaying a complete outline on which the complete skeleton is shown but only part of the outline itself is given; (b) giving the structure of the outline but not filling in any information; (c) giving students main headings and having them fill in supporting ideas; and (d) having your students prepare a complete outline without assistance.

Additionally, it is important that the outlining exercises you do with students are done with real and meaningful reading and study assignments from your various content texts so that they are not just isolated exercises; rather, they are exercises that will help students develop outlining skills while learning otherwise necessary and relevant content. For those students who need more assistance, you could use small-group and one-to-one sessions to promote their development of outlining skills. As can be seen, the teaching outlining procedure involves scaffolded instruction, with the teacher providing maximum support in the beginning and gradually withdrawing support as the students take on more and more responsibility. Moore et al. (2003) refer to this as fading.

When using fading, the teacher demonstrates what she or he expects students to do, fades out assistance as students practice the task with the teacher's help, and finally fades out more as the teacher provides opportunities for independent application. Fading moves from demonstration to guided practice to independent application "as teachers fade out and students fade in" (Moore et al. 2003, p. 26). The idea is to eventually develop student independence. This fading can be applied to all study-learning skills and strategies instruction and is recommended for learning other study-learning skills and strategies in this book.

Underlining and Student Glossing

Underlining and student glossing are related and useful study-learning skills. The primary objective of underlining is to select the most important concepts and information in text and then underline or highlight them for future reference. The primary objective of student glossing is to select the most important concepts and information in text and then make margin notes about them for future reference. (Refer back to Figure 3–7 for an example of student glossing.)

Of course, some students have a tendency to underline or highlight more information than they should, thus negating the benefit of having only the most important information marked in the text for future study references. Without teacher modeling and demonstration (as in Figure 3–6) students will not know how much is too much when they try to gloss their own texts. Some research studies (e.g., Blanchard 1985) have shown underlining to be the most popular organizational study skill, even though other research has presented mixed results in determining its effectiveness when compared with other strategies (Harris and Sipay 1990; McAndrew 1983).

Poostay (1984) suggested that teachers use the following instructional sequence to assist students in developing their underlining skills:

1. Copy a selection of 100 to 150 words.

2. Preview the selection, then underline key concepts. Include five to seven key concepts per 100 words.

3. Make copies of the underlined selection for your students.

4. As you read a portion of the selection, call students' attention to each underlined concept.

5. Demonstrate and discuss how and why each concept was selected.

6. Read the selection again and ask students to predict the content of the selection using only the underlined concepts.

7. Collect the underlined selection, give out the original source and ask the students to read it.

8. Use unaided and aided recall strategies to check the students' comprehension of the selection.

9. Allow students to practice on other selections, and then encourage them to use this technique on their own.

I have developed a similar instructional sequence for helping your students see how they can use their own glossings to study and learn from their content reading materials. The steps are detailed for your future use:

1. Copy a selection from a textbook of at least four paragraphs in length that all the students are currently using in class for content study and display it using your overhead projector.

2. Read the entire selection aloud to your students as they follow along.

3. Use teacher marginal glossing (as in Figure 3–6). Model, mark, and gloss the first paragraph or part of the displayed selection, as you explain to students why you are noting certain concepts or information.

4. Next, solicit students' input, suggestions, and rationales to mark and gloss the second part (or second paragraph) of the displayed selection, reiterating what they told you to mark and their reasons.

5. Let individual students (volunteers) come forward to mark and gloss and explain their rationales on the third part (or third paragraph) of the displayed selection.

6. Suggest that students work in cooperative groups to mark and gloss the fourth part (or paragraph) in the selection. Leave the overhead material on display and give each student in the cooperative group a copy of the fourth part of the selection to finish.

7. When they are done, have volunteers from the cooperative groups come forward and mark the fourth part on the overhead selection, explaining their group rationale.

8. When the entire selection is marked, suggest that the class help you look back at the glossings, and on chart paper, solicit a list of important glossed concepts and information that might help students on a test or is important for them to know.

9. Solicit students' ideas as to the benefits of students glossing their own important reading materials.

As noted in the previous section, again the teacher uses scaffolding or fading to teach these skills. Students are encouraged to use these skills on their own as study-learning tools whenever they feel ready, but the teacher is available to fade in support when students need or want it.

Note Taking and Note Making

Note taking and note making are important study-learning skills (Flippo 2000). Note taking can be very useful to students as they listen to information presented in teacher lectures and discussions (Armbruster 2000) and as they read and study their textbooks (Caverly, Orlando, and Mullen 2000). Extensive review of the research on note taking has shown that the actual process of taking the notes can help note takers learn and remember information; additionally, the notes themselves will preserve the information for later use by the students (Armbruster 2000). However, students must be taught to take notes that are appropriate to the demands being placed on them (Caverly, Orlando, and Mullen 2000). Notes seem helpful to the extent that they contain information that will be tested, but what students do with their notes is equally important. Students need to be able to cognitively process the noted information, encoding it in the same way that they will need to use it on a test (Armbruster 2000).

In *TestWise* (Flippo 2000), I develop many ideas and strategies for note taking and note making. Emphasis is placed on the importance of students' note-making activities to assist their internalization and encoding of the material to be learned. I further suggest that students develop skill in condensing their study notes by rewriting them several times. Each time the notes are condensed further, students have to redetermine what is most important and synthesize the information further. Flippo (2000) could be consulted for descriptions of note-taking and note-making strategies that include organizing notes into topic cards, lists, outlines, and diagrams and organizing class notes, condensing notes, and studying with notes.

Kiewra (1984) delineated a sequence of steps to facilitate note-taking success that included: (1) using effective note-taking techniques during class; (2) taking extensive notes at first; (3) employing paraphrasing or summarizing note-taking procedures; (4) revising notes as quickly as possible after they are taken; (5) reviewing notes before the next class; and (6) incorporating externally provided notes in all note-taking and reviewing procedures.

Although many schemes and formats are provided in the literature for taking and making notes, one is illustrated based on the suggestions I develop in *TestWise* (Flippo 2000). See Figure 4–1. Using this format, students can fold and use standard-sized lined looseleaf notebook paper or they can use stenographer's notebook pages in order to divide their

Figure 4–1   A note-taking and note-making format

Class or Unit: _____   Date: _____

General Topic _____

Subtopic _____   Notes: _____

_____

_____

_____

_____

_____

_____

_____

_____

_____

New Subtopic _____   Notes: _____

_____

_____

_____

_____

_____

_____

_____

_____

New Subtopic _____   Notes: _____

_____

_____

_____

_____

_____

_____

_____

_____

paper for note-taking purposes. Record the name of the class or unit of study and the date at the top of the first page of each day's notes. Use the first line of the left column to jot down the general topic heading. Then also in the left column list the subtopic heading. In the right-hand column next to the subtopic, list the related notes, facts, ideas, and concepts for the subtopic that are given in class or in the assigned readings. Skip at least a couple of lines of space between each set of topics and notes as they change. Make sure to list new general topics and/or subtopics in the left columns when the topic has changed. Take notes on the front side of the page only so that you can more easily reorganize your notes by topics when studying for a test. (For example, at the end of a unit of study, students can easily cut the pages of their notes apart and regroup them by topics/subtopics.)

Reflection Activity 4.2

What ideas could you suggest for developing the outlining, underlining, and student glossing skills, as well as note-taking and note-making skills, of elementary and middle school students? Also, how would you suggest that fading be used to provide the necessary supports for student learning while fostering the development of independence?

Specialized Study-Learning Skills

Students need other various specialized study-learning skills to successfully carry out and complete different study-learning assignments and to use and learn information obtained from the books and other materials they must use. These specialized study-learning skills are discussed next. As with other study-learning skills discussed in this book, it is important that teachers make use of modeling, demonstrating, and fading instruction to provide the support students need as well as the opportunities for independent learning development.

Using Parts of Textbooks

To use textbooks effectively, students need a good working knowledge of the resources found in a textbook and where and how to use them to find certain types of information. For example, your students should know that the table of contents is in the front of the text and that it is useful in getting an idea of what is in each chapter. They also need to know that the index is usually in the back of the textbook and can be helpful in locating more specific details and topical information. Understanding what the glossary, the title and copyright pages, and the bibliography or references are for can facilitate your students' research and other information-gathering needs.

Teachers can ask students to use these various text resources as part of their content-reading assignments, modeling where each can be found and how to use them. For example, when beginning the rainforest unit, Mrs. Argueta had students review the table of contents in their text and guess in what chapter the information on rainforests would be found. Students were asked to explain their rationales for guessing. Then, using the table of contents, students found the page numbers and turned to the indicated chapters to confirm or disprove their guesses. She also asked students to check the index at the back of the book to see whether "rainforests" were cited on any particular pages. Students then looked on those pages to see what was said about rainforests. Mrs. Argueta wanted students to know how to cite a reference, so she showed them how to cite their texts using the title and copyright pages. When students were introduced to new vocabulary in their text reading on rainforests, she suggested and modeled use of the glossary. Finally, when she wanted students to notice the bibliography at the end of the text chapter, she asked them to see whether they could find a list of other books and sources with information on rainforests. She showed students how to scan the bibliography for appropriate sources students might want to find to give them more information on rainforests.

Reading Graphically Displayed Information

Graphically displayed information skills include reading graphs, tables, charts, and maps. The importance of these skills is reinforced by research that has suggested that both children and adults remember pictures of objects better than names of objects (Levin 1976), as well as by recognition that graphical literacy is an important communication tool and deserves a place in the school curriculum (Fry 1981).

Teachers can enhance students' skills at reading and using graphically displayed information by more often using and discussing the maps, tables, and other graphic displays found in students' textbooks. These displays, which are sometimes ignored by teachers, can be used to make the content materials more interesting and meaningful for students. Students can also be encouraged, with the teacher's support, to do their own meaningful research and develop their own graphic displays to share their research findings. This helps students understand the use of graphic materials better and helps them to understand the relationships more clearly (Devine 1987; Hoyt 2002; Moore et al. 2003; Flippo 2003). In my reading assessment and instruction book (Flippo 2003), I present several of these ideas for developing graph- and table-reading skills and strategies by using student-generated questions and research.

Flippo and Frounfelker (1988) developed a map-reading activity that emphasizes basic map-reading concepts, vocabulary, and symbol interpretation for middle-grade elementary students and encourages them to self-assess their understandings and knowledge (see Figure 4–2). First the teacher introduces the subject of map study and displays a variety of maps. Then the teacher gives each student the self-assessment sheet and asks one student to volunteer to read a question aloud from the sheet. After allowing time for all students to answer the question for themselves, the teacher has another volunteer answer and tell how she or he arrived at the answer. If the student gives a full and accurate answer, the teacher says, "You knew the answer," and tells the other students, if they responded similarly, to check the "I knew answer" space following the question on the self-assessment sheet. If an answer is only partially accurate, the teacher says, "You knew part of the answer. Keep thinking, maybe you will get the rest of it." Other students with

Figure 4–2   Self-assessment of sample map-reading skills

Self Assessment of Sample Map-Reading Skills

Questions	I knew the answer	I knew part of the answer	I did not know the answer	Unknown words
1. What is a map?	_____	_____	_____	_____
2. What is a compass rose?	_____	_____	_____	_____
3. What are the four cardinal directions?	_____	_____	_____	_____
4. What is a map scale?	_____	_____	_____	_____
5. What is a map key or legend?	_____	_____	_____	_____
6. What are symbols used in a map key?	_____	_____	_____	_____
7. What is a map grid?	_____	_____	_____	_____
8. What does parallel mean?	_____	_____	_____	_____
9. What does perpendicular mean?	_____	_____	_____	_____
10. What are coordinates?	_____	_____	_____	_____
11. What is a political map?	_____	_____	_____	_____
12. What is a boundary?	_____	_____	_____	_____
13. What is a capital?	_____	_____	_____	_____
14. Name one common kind of map that is a political map.	_____	_____	_____	_____
15. What is a physical map?	_____	_____	_____	_____
16. How are things or features shown on a physical map?	_____	_____	_____	_____
17. What is an elevation map?	_____	_____	_____	_____
18. What are contour lines?	_____	_____	_____	_____
19. What is a demographic map?	_____	_____	_____	_____
20. Name two things you can learn from a demographic map.	_____	_____	_____	_____

From R. F. Flippo and C. R. Frounfelker, III, (1988), "Teach Map Reading Through Self Assessment." *The Reading Teacher, 42*(3): 259. Reprinted by permission of Rona F. Flippo and the International Reading Association, Copyright by the International Reading Association, Newark, Delaware.

similar answers would check the "I knew part of the answer" space. The teacher solicits a more complete answer from volunteers. If the answer is inaccurate, the teacher says "You don't know the answer, but it was a good try." Students with similar responses would check the "I did not know the answer" space. Again, the teacher solicits volunteers to come up with the correct answer. As other questions are read, students write any words they do not know in the right column of the sheet. These words can later serve as individual vocabulary research lists. When all the questions have been reviewed and checked, the teacher can use the information to make instructional decisions. Later, after instruction has been provided, students can reassess their understanding using the same procedure.

Flippo and Frounfelker (1988) indicated that this sharing and clarifying of information, along with the self-assessment activity, enhances learning and motivates students. Teachers can develop their own similar activities for table- and graph-reading skills and to enhance skills for reading and using other graphic displays.

Skimming and Scanning

The specialized study-reading skills of skimming and scanning enable readers to preview material, to search for specific details, and to develop a general impression of the material. Skimming material involves a brisk reading of that material to form an overall general impression. Scanning, however, involves very rapid reading with the task of searching for specific details or pieces of information. Both skills are used singularly or in combination to read and study content.

Fry (1989) has developed materials for teaching and helping upper-grade elementary students to develop skimming and scanning skills. However, classroom teachers can use their own materials if they have some guidance as to how to proceed. Using the following procedures, you can demonstrate and provide practice to teach your students these important specialized skills:

1. Select full excerpts of text that are at least 1,000 to 1,500 words long. (It is best to use text that students will have to read anyway as part of your content reading plans.)

2. Demonstrate the skills of skimming and scanning by modeling how you do it with the selected text projected on an overhead projector. (Explain what you are doing when you skim: You are trying to quickly review the material to see whether it is what you were looking for and to see whether you need to read it more carefully. Explain what you are doing when you scan: You are reading the material rapidly and looking for specific information.)

3. Pose some questions about the material and ask students to scan with you to search for the specific answers. (Work through the selection with the students helping you find the specific information.)

4. Using a second excerpt of the same length, give all students a copy with some specific questions and let students practice skimming and scanning in small cooperative learning groups.

5. For variety and more practice opportunities, students can skim and scan a variety of materials (e.g., lists, indexes, newspaper articles, schedules, tables, TV guides, material found on the Internet).

As you can see, skimming and scanning needs to be modeled and taught, but once learned, the teacher can fade out and let students use their skimming and scanning techniques as another study-learning tool.

Adjusting Reading Rate

Students need to be able to vary their reading rates according to specific purposes and materials. Often students will instead read all materials at the same rate, which results in sporadic comprehension of important text information. This seems to be more prevalent when they read different types of content materials, such as math, science, social studies, or literature texts. In general, the more technical the information and vocabulary, the slower the rate your students may need to use. However, the purpose for reading the material should also help students moderate their rates.

Flippo and Lecheler (1987) developed a procedure to encourage intermediate-grade elementary students to be more aware of their reading rates and to adjust their rates and concentration for different materials based on the difficulty of the materials. This procedure causes students to become aware of how fast they can read something and still understand it. It requires them to decide whether they can read certain material *slowly, moderately,* or *fast*—words that youngsters can easily understand. I recommend that you utilize this procedure and develop activities using curriculum materials from your own classroom to develop rate awareness and adjustment proficiency. The procedure is outlined for your use:

1. Tell students what you would like them to do by providing the reason: "Because some materials are more difficult to read than others, your reading rate shouldn't always be the same. It should vary."

2. Use several examples to illustrate what you mean and explain why you would read these slowly, moderately, or fast.

3. Ask, "Why are some materials read faster than others?" List students' responses on the board.

4. Ask students to suggest materials that they would read slowly, moderately, or fast, but emphasize that understanding the material is still important. Write these suggested materials and the rates students provide on the board.

5. Ask individual students to explain their rationales for the suggestions they made in number 4. Accept individual reasons. What might be difficult for one student to read and understand might not be for another.

6. Ask students to find passages and excerpts from varieties of textbooks and materials you use in class, read them silently, and then give rates they suggest for themselves. Establish this as an ongoing assignment.

7. Allow many opportunities for students to share their passages and excerpts, suggested rates, and reasons. This can be done over an extended period of time in small or large groups. This helps students develop their individual metacognitive rate awareness.

Students' abilities to adjust their reading rates while at the same time reading for meaning are part of their overall *fluency* (Flippo 2003, pp. 90–92). Helping students develop an awareness of the purpose of the reading, the difficulty of the material to be read, and the maximum rate they are able to read and understand the material should enhance their study-learning skills, their fluency, *and* their confidence as learners.

Reflection Activity 4.3

How can a teacher help his or her students develop, practice, and use the study-learning skills and strategies that would be most effective for their assignments? How can students be encouraged to become independent learners who challenge themselves to succeed in their studies and to accept more responsibility for their own learning?

Study-Learning Skills and Strategies: A Summary

In summary, study-learning skills and strategies are worth teaching. Students need these skills to pursue and do the many learning tasks and assignments that elementary and upper-grade teachers assign. However, like all other teaching, study-learning skills and strategies should be embedded in the authentic content curriculum of your classroom and should be intrinsically motivating to students. They should be presented to be used for real purposes, real situations, and in the pursuit of real and interesting assignments. Guthrie and Pressley (1992, p. 257) reviewed and summarized the research relative to cognitive competence and indicated the following:

1. Students comprehend text more fully and remember the information longer if they view the texts as a means for learning an idea or

gaining an experience, as opposed to objects to be understood and recalled.

2. Cognitive strategies are learned more rapidly when reading goals are immersed in substantive and intrinsic purposes.

3. Students learn to search for ideas and locate information across a variety of texts and references most efficiently when the texts are provided as tools and resources among other resources for learning.

4. Students will read more independently and voluntarily when reading is part of a substantive, intrinsically oriented goal, rather than just for teacher-directed purposes.

Try It Out

1. Using their actual text assignments in science or social studies, have students create a glossary of terms using reference materials.

2. Using the actual topics in their social studies readings, have students use both electronic and nonelectronic research and reference materials (including search engines, email, and other features of the Internet) to write a short book or skit on the topic of their choice.

3. After modeling and scaffolding outlining, have partners or small groups create a Website for a science or social studies topic and outline the information. Then using Inspiration software, recreate the Website and compare their outlines to the one generated by the software program. Use the outlines to write summaries of the text.

4. Long after elementary and middle school, your students will need to use reference and research skills, organizational skills, outlining, underlining and student glossing, note taking and note making, parts of textbooks, graphically displayed information, skimming and scanning, and know how to adjust their reading rate. Helping them to understand the varying situations where the ability to use these skills and strategies will present itself could help them understand the relevance of learning to effectively use them now. Encourage discussion of these study-learning skills and strategies, asking students for examples of the kinds of things that can be affected by someone knowing how to use them *or* not knowing how to use them. Students can also develop skits to show the relevance of these skills.

Test-Preparation and Test-Taking Skills

5

Test-preparation skills and strategies actually involve use of most of the other study-learning skills explained in Chapter 4. Application of study-learning skills is really what good test preparation is all about, and in *TestWise* (Flippo 2000), I recommend many strategies for helping students use the various study-learning skills to study for and otherwise prepare for upcoming essay and objective tests. Highlights of these are presented and explained in this chapter.

Simpson (1984) indicated that when students have had little or no instruction in the use of study and learning strategies, their comprehension of content materials in middle school and beyond can be seriously affected. Weinstein and Mayer (1986) summarized some of the major categories of study-learning skills and strategies, which I further develop with examples of elementary classroom learning tasks in Figure 5–1 in order to show the relationship between the study-learning skills and test study and preparation strategies. When students know how to learn, they will be able to have control over their learning and studying.

Figure 5–1   Categories of study-learning strategies

Categories of Study-Learning Strategies

(Each category includes strategies and practices that influence aspects of the encoding process which facilitate one or more types of learning outcome and performance.)

Rehearsal/strategies for basic learning tasks—such as repeating the names of items in an ordered list. Common school tasks in this category included remembering the order of the planets from the sun and the order in which the major battles of the Civil War occured.

Rehearsal/strategies for complex learning tasks—such as copying, underlining or highlighting the material presented in class. Common school tasks in this category include underlining the main events in a story or copying the most important ideas from the text about the causes of the Civil War.

Elaboration strategies for basic learning tasks—such as forming a mental image or sentence relating the items in each pair for a paired-associate list of words. Common school tasks in this category include forming a phrase or sentence relating the name of a state and its major agricultural product, or forming a mental image of a scene described by a poem.

Elaboration strategies for complex tasks—such as paraphrasing, summarizing, or describing how new information relates to existing knowledge. Common school tasks in this category include creating an analogy between the operation of a school and the operation of the government, or relating the information presented about the planets of the solar system to the information presented about the sun.

Organizational strategies for basic learning tasks—such as grouping or ordering to-be-learned items from a list or a section of text. Common school tasks in this category include organizing new vocabulary words into categories for various parts of speech, or creating a chronological listing of the events that led up to the Declaration of Independence.

Organizational strategies for complex tasks—such as outlining a section of a chapter or creating a hierarchy. Common school tasks in this category include outlining assigned chapters in the textbook, or creating a diagram to show the relationship among the various forms of life in the rainforest.

Comprehension monitoring strategies—such as checking for understanding. Common school tasks in this category include using self-questioning to check understanding of the material presented in class and using the questions in a study guide to guide one's reading focus while studying a textbook.

Affective strategies—such as being ready, sure of oneself, and relaxed, to help overcome test anxiety. Common school tasks in this category include reducing external distractions by studying in a quiet place or using relaxation techniques as necessary during a test.

Derived and developed from C. E. Weinstein and E. Mayer (1986), "The Teaching of Learning Strategies," in M. C. Wittrock, ed., *Handbook of Research on Teaching,* 3d ed., pp. 315–17. New York: Macmillan.

Teaching Test-Preparation and Test-Taking Skills

Some teachers may assume that students will develop efficient test-preparation and test-taking skills as they mature and may not teach these skills to students. Unfortunately, many students never learn the skills. Flippo and Borthwick (1982) noted that test-taking instruction is not part of most teacher education programs. If teachers were never taught test-taking and test-wiseness strategies, they may not know how to teach these strategies to their students. It is important for teachers to assist students in developing the ability to apply systematic procedures in studying for and taking tests. The research literature supports the idea that special instruction in preparing for and taking tests can lead to better test results (Flippo, Becker, and Wark 2000).

Test-Wiseness

Learning to be test-wise depends on learning how to apply different strategies to different types of tests, as well as other important aspects of study preparation. These aspects include the following (Flippo 2000):

1. organizing study materials for a test

2. actually studying for the specific test

3. knowing how to use various test-taking cues and understanding the different characteristics of different types of tests

4. actually taking the test using time-management organization, knowledge of topic information, and internal cues in the test

Test-Preparation Suggestions

A summary of test-preparation suggestions from my own book (Flippo 2000) and Pauk's classic work in its seventh edition (2001) can provide you with a listing that could be given to your upper-elementary-grade students in the form of a checklist. The checklist could consist of the following points:

1. Review lecture and reading notes periodically.

2. Plan a definite exam study schedule and stick to it.

3. Prepare and study a master outline of the test subject (an informal, condensed version of all your notes). Making an outline or master set of important notes is an excellent review. Recite to yourself the facts and ideas related to each item in the outline or notes.

4. Besides memorizing, synthesizing, and analyzing, try to see the inter-relationships. (Examine material from your own point of view.)

5. Ask about the type of test that is to be administered. Make up test questions or an exam, take it, and grade it.

6. Remember that the best way to know a concept is to be able to state it correctly in your own words. Study with this objective in mind.

7. Pay special attention to important points and ideas. Make a list of hard-to-remember facts and information. Note cards are a good idea. Repeatedly summarize, write, further condense, rewrite, and recite important points noted on your cards.

8. Do not be afraid to cram. Have a final review the night before an exam and continue to review and recite important information right up until exam time. (Although cramming sometimes carries a negative connotation, I have emphasized that cramming is just intense studying, and in fact, good students do it all the time (Flippo 2000, pp. 60–61).

Objective and Essay Tests

Students need to be aware of the demands of various objective tests, as well as essay tests, to effectively prepare for them. Additionally, knowing in advance what they will be expected to do when faced with these different test formats will help students conserve their time and more effectively work through their tests. Knowing the material is only one part of doing well on a test. This section provides the basic information for each type of objective test and for essay test questions. Practice using these test formats, with content that your students will actually have to know, is a good way to help them not only learn the material, but also be more successful test takers.

Objective Tests

Objective tests usually consist of true and false, multiple-choice, matching, and fill-in questions. True-false are absolute statements, in that you either answer a question "true" or "false." A strategy to remember is that when a true-false statement is only partly true, the answer is false. Also, absolute modifiers are words that tend to appear in false statements. Examples of such words are *always, all,* and *only.* However, qualifiers such as *frequently, some,* and *many* tend to more often appear in true statements.

Multiple-choice questions are incomplete statements followed by possible answers. The question is referred to as the stem and the choices are called options. A question usually has four or five answer choices, with one answer being the correct option and the others the distractors. One strategy your students could use for answering multiple-choice questions is to eliminate as many of the distractors as possible, and to analyze the remaining stem and possible options as though they were true-false questions. In *TestWise* (Flippo 2000, pp. 118–21 and 126–28), I recommend the following techniques that should help students select the best multiple-choice option:

1. Read the stem and anticipate the answer before you look at the options.

2. Lightly mark in pencil a T or F by the options as you review each; only the Ts are usually possibilities.

3. Use cues in the options, for instance:

    a. The most general alternative is often the most encompassing of the choices and may be the correct choice.

b. Two similar alternatives often have nearly the same meaning; both cannot be correct unless it is a key word that is different.

c. The use of two alternatives of opposite meaning often indicates that one of them is correct; when teachers make up alternatives for questions, an antonym for the correct answer is often the first thing that comes to mind.

d. "None" or "all-of-the-above" alternatives can be eliminated or selected by noting whether you put all Fs or all Ts by the options.

4. Using these and other cues and your knowledge of the material, eliminate as many of the options as possible, and if more than one option is still left, take your best guess from the remaining options.

Shepherd (1998) has suggested that teachers provide the following procedures to students for answering matching and fill-in questions.

Matching Questions

1. Examine both lists to understand the types of items you are to match.

2. Use one list as the starting place to make all matches.

3. If one list has longer statements, use it as the starting place to make all matches.

4. Match first those items that you are certain are matches.

5. Cross out items as you are able to match them.

6. Use logical clues to match any items you are uncertain about.

Fill-In Questions

1. Decide what type of answer is wanted.

2. When a question contains two consecutive blanks, provide a two-word answer.

3. When a blank is preceded by the word *an,* provide an answer that begins with a vowel (*a, e, i, o* or *u*).

When applying test-wiseness strategies to matching and fill-in type of questions, you should encourage your students to also use their own prior knowledge of the particular subject matter under consideration to monitor their choice of responses, along with the preceding suggestions.

Essay Tests

Essay tests differ from objective tests in that the answers must be constructed rather than recognized, and these answers will be graded in a more subjective manner than those on objective tests. The advantage of essay tests is that they maximize the use of the knowledge and understandings students have. Students' success also depends on developing and using their understandings of the content materials, organizing that content, and writing clear, well-developed responses that rely on their understandings and organization. To prepare for an essay test, I have recommended the following advice, which could be explained and demonstrated to upper-elementary students (Flippo 2000, pp. 62–81):

1. Use your notes and knowledge of the content that will be tested to predict the types of questions you will be asked.

2. Predict the questions and practice writing answers to them, using your notes and other resources you gathered for study. (Even if the questions you predict are not exactly the same as those on the test, the process of predicting and answering questions will help you learn the material more thoroughly.)

Figure 5–2, derived from Flippo (2000), displays the kinds of questions and the key words and phrases that signal various types of essay questions and the responses that are required. Using your own class content materials and notes, your students can practice predicting and answering potential essay exam questions.

A strategy that students can use for studying for an essay or objective test is the use of mnemonic acronyms. The mnemonic acronym "COW" can be used to remember the three steps for taking essay tests. *Mnemonic* means "to help the memory" and *acronym* is a word made

Figure 5–2	Kinds of essay questions	
Kinds of questions	**Key words**	**Phrases that signal questions**
Short-answer	List	
	Name	
	Define	
	Identify	
Long-answer	Trace	Describe the steps in...
		Trace the development of...
		Trace the events leading up to...
		Outline the history of...
	Compare and contrast	Tell how _____ and _____ are alike or different.
		Consider the advantages or disadvantages of...
		Compare and contrast _____ and _____ .
		Show the similarities and differences between _____ and _____ .
	Discuss	Discuss the significance of the problems of...
		What is the relationship between _____ and _____ ?
		Discuss the effect of...
		Discuss the role of...

Derived from R. F. Flippo (2000), *TestWise: Strategies for Success in Taking Tests,* 2d ed. pp. 62–81. Grand Rapids, MI: Good Apple an imprint of McGraw-Hill Children's Publishing.

from the initial letters of other words. "COW" stands for: *C*onstruct; *O*rganize; and *W*rite. Mnemonic devices are also used in making up sentences, but this strategy should be used selectively.

Finally, the key to receiving a good grade on an essay test is being able to organize ideas. An exam taker needs to develop a line of thinking and use examples to illustrate a theme. Some students know all the facts, write everything they know, and yet receive little credit for their essay answers. Studying facts in isolation, failing to understand the facts, not following directions, and not dividing test time properly are common errors. For example, your students can write a mini-outline for each essay question. The mini-outline briefly lists the major points intended for their answers. Other strategies for responses to essay tests are to answer the question directly, reflect on the organization of the potential answer, use facts to support statements, use examples to help clarify points made, and in conclusion to be sure the essay answer is organized with thoughts clearly exemplified. In reflecting and self-monitoring their answers, students can determine whether their conclusion summarizes their response.

Practice for the Test

In *TestWise* (Flippo 2000), I provide practice on various study skills and strategies as part of test-preparation and test-taking strategies by applying the study skills to actual test-preparation situations. Many test-preparation strategies include skills and strategies that teachers may traditionally teach as part of their usual study-skills instruction (e.g., note taking, outlining, summarizing). However, when teaching your students these skills and strategies as part of their test-taking preparation, you are providing a tangible purpose for students to become accomplished in important related study-learning skills. Furthermore, appropriate use of the various specialized study skills is important to your students' success in the various study-learning assignments they undertake.

One way to provide an opportunity to practice for an important upcoming test *and* give your students an incentive to review the material that they have been reading and learning is the Fake Pop Quiz (FPQ). I have used the FPQ with students of all ages. Their feedback has indicated that they liked taking it and they believed that it helped them learn the material as well as get ready for the test. They even thought it was *fair* to allow them the chance to "practice" in this way before taking the actual test.

Below are some basic considerations to bear in mind when preparing and giving FPQs; note that they can be done with any of the various objective formats or types of essay questions delineated in this chapter.

1. The FPQ is a simulation of the *real* upcoming test, but it is not necessarily the actual, real test.

2. The FPQ can be open book or closed book, depending on the teacher's goals in giving it.

3. Design FPQs that give students an opportunity to review and reinforce the learning of the information you (the teacher) believe is most important to be learned.

4. If possible, design FPQs that simulate the format and content of the real upcoming test.

5. Tell students that their FPQ scores will not *count* or affect their grade in any way.

6. Introduce it by saying something like, "Today we are going to have a fake pop quiz on the rainforest material we've been reading. The FPQ will not affect your grade, but it will help you see how well you know the information in the rainforest material. It will also help you get ready for the real test on this material which we will be taking on _____."

7. After students complete the FPQ, let them score it themselves or allow them to work in small groups doing peer evaluations. You can allow them to refer to the material itself to find the correct answers or you can provide the answers.

8. Understand that the FPQ is designed to reinforce rather than *test* learning, and its purpose is to stimulate interest (Readance, Bean, and Baldwin 2001).

What is your professional opinion concerning teaching students how to study for and take tests? Do you feel that somehow this is not appropriate or not ethical? Several researchers and practitioners have indicated that they believe that students have a right to test-preparation and test-taking instruction, and that success in test taking is an important aspect of school, often affecting students' entire lives (Flippo 2000, Flippo and Borthwick 1982, Pauk 2001, Shepherd 1998). What has been your experience with this issue?

Test-Preparation and Test-Taking Skills: A Summary

Test-taking and test-preparation skills will continue to be important to students as they move up through the grades. Students of all grades and at all levels of their education are required to take tests. These tests will be part of the evaluations of their school learning as well as the entrance requirement to various special programs, postsecondary opportunities, other training programs, and licensure credentialing. Just like all other things they learn, learning and perfecting these skills occurs gradually over time. It is the role of the elementary through middle school teacher to ensure that students have an opportunity to develop these skills. The content classroom provides a natural setting in which this can happen.

1. After practicing with the class various study-learning skills (from Chapter 4) and test-preparation strategies (reviewed in this chapter), allow students to form cooperative study groups. Each member of a group should use the study-learning and test-preparation skills he or she prefers. For example, while each student reviews his own notes and further prepares his notes for studying, one may use note making, another outlining, and another might make note cards. After they have all prepared the information individually, students share and compare their notes with their group, explaining why their particular notes and organization of them are important, and the group discusses relationships between each of their ideas.

2. Using test-preparation and test-taking strategies, allow students to individually or in cooperative groups create their own quiz or test (either objective or essay format). Students should decide what information is important to know and can decide how it should be tested. After the teacher reviews the quiz for content and clarity, have students switch quizzes with a partner or with another cooperative group and take each other's tests. Students can then grade the tests they created by looking up answers in text or notes.

3. Prepare a Fake Pop Quiz (FPQ) for your class. After the students complete it and the responses are evaluated (note, see the suggestion for doing this in number 7 on page 80), encourage students to discuss the merits of taking a FPQ. Was it helpful? How did it help? What else should they do to prepare for the upcoming "real" test?

4. For upper-elementary and middle-school students, you might like to suggest a debate: Divide the class into two groups (allowing students to select the "side" they want to be on). Have one side discuss the reasons that students should be taught test-preparation and test-taking strategies and the other group why they should not. After ample discussion time, allow the "sides" to debate their reasoning.

Strategy Systems for Reading, Studying, and Learning

6

I n this chapter, several specific study-reading and learning strategy systems that elementary through middle school students and their teachers can use to help students read, learn from, and study text are presented. Devine and Kania (2003) explain that *study systems* result when teachers and researchers have combined two or more study strategies into a *system* designed to assist students to understand, learn, remember, and/or apply new information, knowledge, and procedures. These strategy systems can be helpful tools for students as they develop skills and strategies for learning how to learn.

Johnston (1985) has emphasized the difference between "teaching strategies" and "learning strategies" and advocated that teachers transfer their efforts to assisting students in learning various learning strategies. When students become involved in a learning strategy, they are more likely to effectively use the strategy independently and in varied situations. As you introduce the study-reading and learning strategy or system to your students, you will want to model the correct usage and application of each strategy, scaffolding as necessary, so that your students will gain an understanding of its use and effectiveness with various text materials. It is also important to give students an appropriate amount of time to practice and to receive feedback from you in order to enable them to use these strategies effectively. However, remember to always let students practice and apply the study-reading strategies to materials they really need to read or really want to learn in order to do their school assignments and other personal research, rather than to just "practice materials." As emphasized previously, making schoolwork authentic and assignments real and meaningful is an important part of the classroom teacher's role.

However, Caverly, Orlando, and Mullen (2000) caution that *understanding the unique and combined effects of the following four variables is crucial for understanding the effectiveness of any given study-reading and learning strategy system:*

- the student
- the material
- the instruction
- the task demand

They indicate that "the question is not whether [a particular] study-reading strategy is successful. Rather it is *where, when, and under what conditions* a strategy is successful" (p. 106).

Readence, Bean, and Baldwin (2001) suggest that it is best to select and introduce reading, study, and learning strategies that have the following characteristics:

1. The strategy helps students focus attention on important information.

2. The strategy provides students with meaningful study and learning goals.

3. The strategy helps students organize information.

4. The strategy encourages students to read, study, and/or learn.

5. The strategy encourages deep processing of information.

Each of the strategies or strategy systems presented in this chapter meets these suggested characteristics. Additionally, each of them can be taught to elementary and middle school students. Of course, teachers will need to model, scaffold, ask metacognitive questions, and provide examples and ample practice with appropriate materials suitable to the curricula and assignments for the grades in which the students are in. Also, teachers will see that some strategies might be more effective with certain subject areas and materials than others, as well as with certain students and assignment demands.

K-W-L

This strategy, developed by Ogle (1986), can be used, at first, as a teaching strategy; but later, once students get the idea and see how they can apply it to anything they want to learn, it can also be an effective learning strategy. It has been a favorite in my teacher education classes and workshops over the years. K-W-L is designed to activate students' prior knowledge when interacting with expository text and to increase their level of interest in reading, studying, and learning about selected topics. The three steps in this strategy are as follows:

1. *K—What I Know.* The students collaboratively respond to a concept presented before they read a selection or begin a new unit of learning. You record their ideas on the chalkboard, poster board, etc., in order to use them as a beginning point for discussion. (Later, once students *know* this learning strategy, they can use notebook paper or a worksheet you can design to work through the K-W-L steps on their own.) After working through the K step, collaboratively generate categories from their responses to help students better understand the text or content they will be learning about.

2. *W—What Do I Want to Learn?* Students develop questions that highlight their area of interest as a result of the activities in the first step. Students then read the selection or begin learning the new material.

3. *L—What I Learned.* After completing the text selection or unit of learning, students list what they have learned, check this against their questions, and answer any remaining questions.

K-W-L is a strategy that can be used with all grade levels. Additionally, variations of it can help students focus on such things as "What now do I still want to/need to learn more about?" and "Where can I find the additional needed information?" Readers may also want to see Hayes (1992) for his examples of a similar strategy, known as *Metacognitive Modeling*, which was conceived by Heller (1986).

Teachers could easily add -WN (what now) and -W (where) columns to their K-W-L procedures. For instance, see Figure 6–1 for an example of a K-W-L worksheet with my suggested additions. Also, Mandeville (1994) suggested another variation, an *Affect* column. Using an affect (A) column, students could answer questions about their learning such as "Was this interesting to learn? Why or why not? Is this information I learned important? Why or why not?" Thus, using Mandeville's idea, this variation strategy could be called *KWLA*.

Reciprocal Teaching and Learning

Reciprocal Teaching is a strategy for helping students comprehend and learn from their texts. The students take turns leading the instruction after the teacher has modeled the full procedure. The strategy includes making predictions, asking questions, summarizing the text, and clarifying difficult concepts in the text. Hayes (1992) provides several examples of this strategy and cites Palincsar and Brown (1986) as the source for the Reciprocal Teaching idea. The steps to this strategy include:

1. The teacher describes the procedure to the students, explaining how it will enhance their comprehension and learning from the text under consideration.

K-W-L-WN-W

Topic: _____

Goal: _____

_____

K What I know:	W What do I want to learn?	L What I learned:	WN What now do I still want to/need to learn?	W Where can I find the additional information?

2. The teacher models each aspect of the procedure, encouraging students to comment on each.

3. During the teacher modeling, students are called on to *make predictions, ask questions, summarize,* and finally *clarify the material* read. This continues until the teacher believes that students understand the procedure and that they are ready to move to the role of teacher.

4. Playing the teacher's role, students one by one monitor other students' success in understanding and learning from the material; the teacher becomes a back-up and resource person providing clues and asking questions only when necessary.

5. The student (who has assumed the role of teacher) asks other individual students to *make predictions* about the text to be read. For example, "What do you think this textbook reading will be about, Tim?" The student (teacher) asks several students the same question.

6. The student (in the role of teacher) then *asks questions.* For example, "Yes, I think you are correct. But what do you think _____ is? Is it similar to _____? Why might this be important to know? Does anyone else have questions?" Again, the student (teacher) continues to probe various students with questions.

7. The student (in the teacher role) next asks students to read the text to themselves to see if it answers any of the questions that were raised.

8. After the reading, the student (teacher) generally *summarizes the text* for the other students. Then the student (teacher) asks individual students to summarize. For example, "Tanya, could you more specifically summarize for us?" Other students are also asked to summarize.

9. Predictions made prior to the reading are recalled and questions that were posed are discussed.

10. The student (teacher) *clarifies* areas or aspects that are not clear. Then the student (teacher) asks individual students to clarify difficult concepts in the text.

This teaching and learning strategy may be used with individual students or groups of students. It is appropriate for all grade levels and subjects of study. Younger students will of course need more support and back-up help from the resource person (the actual classroom teacher); however, in assuming the role of teacher, each student is given an opportunity to activate background knowledge, make hypotheses, actively engage with and seek information from text, integrate text information, and think about and clarify difficult content. These activities should reinforce their learning of the new material under consideration and demonstrate to them how they can learn new information through predicting, questioning, summarizing, and clarifying important material that they must read and learn.

Predict-Test-Conclude

This strategy helps build students' problem-solving skills—helping students formulate and test hypotheses and then make logical conclusions based on their findings. Hayes (1992) explains and presents examples of this strategy and cites Klein (1988) as his source. Predict-Test-Conclude (P-T-C) can be used for many content areas and topics and all grade levels, but Hayes indicates that students must have some background knowledge of the topic before the P-T-C strategy is introduced. The strategy involves three phases:

1. In the *prereading* phase, the teacher asks students to make predictions about the material they will be reading. The teacher stimulates the predictions by asking cause-and-effect or if-then questions, for example, "If _____ happens, then what would the result be for _____?" or "When _____ occurs, what do you expect the result would be?" Students can write or discuss their predictions, and they should be encouraged to explain their reasoning. They may do this in a large group or in small groups.

2. The *reading* phase involves students reading to test their own predictions. As a result, they may alter their predictions or make new ones. Students should write any alterations or new predictions for later discussion.

3. The final phase is *discussion* based on the questions and predictions that were first posed in the prereading phase. Here the teacher asks probing questions in order to help students make connections and draw conclusions. Also, if students altered their predictions or made new ones after the reading, they should be given an opportunity to explain them.

Think-Alouds

One approach to developing metacognitive thinking, promoting comprehension, and enhancing the learning of new materials is utilizing the think-aloud procedure (Kucan and Beck 1997). This is a modeling strategy that involves first the teacher reading aloud from text and verbalizing what comes to mind as he or she reads. Then students practice with the text to be read, understood, and/or learned. Readence, Bean, and Baldwin (2001) provide steps for developing students' think-aloud strategies. Ideally, once learned, students can use this strategy to help themselves individually learn from textual readings. This procedure may be utilized with narrative as well as expository text.

1. Initially, select a passage of between 100 and 300 words from students' assigned reading.

2. Prepare comments for the think-alouds you will share with students as you read aloud to them from the selected text.

3. Explain to the students what you are going to be doing, letting them know that you wish to show them how you think when you read.

4. Read the selected passage(s) to the class and insert your prepared think-aloud comments as you do so.

5. When you are done, give students an opportunity to ask you questions about how you think or about the think-aloud strategy.

6. Allow students to practice in pairs or in small groups with segments of the text.

7. Allow students who wish to share their think-aloud thoughts with other students in the class to do so.

8. Talk about how this may help us remember or learn what we have read in the text. Allow students to share their thoughts regarding this.

PORPE

PORPE is an essay writing and integrated study strategy developed by Simpson, Stahl, and Hayes (1989). The acronym PORPE stands for each step of the strategy: predict, organize, rehearse, practice, and evaluate. The steps are detailed as follows:

1. First, once the students have completed the reading of the content material to be read, studied, and learned, they are to *predict* potential essay questions.

2. Next, students should outline, map, or use a graphic organizer to *organize* the material they plan to use in order to organize the information for their written response to the predicted question.

3. The third step is to *rehearse* by reciting or writing from memory the organizational structure of the outline, map, or graphic organizer material (see number 2).

4. Next, *practice* by writing from memory an outline for and then an answer to the predicted essay question.

5. The last step is to *evaluate* the practice essay answers. Students may do this independently. The teacher may provide a checklist to help guide students' evaluation; however, I have also allowed cooperative groups and other peer groups of two or more students to develop their own checklists and evaluate each other's essays. I have found that this evaluation and discussion further promotes the understanding and learning of the material.

If you wish to develop such a checklist, see Figure 6–2 for an idea of what one might look like. Use your own ideas to design evaluation checklists that reflect the things you will look for when you evaluate students' actual essay exam responses.

Readence, Bean, and Baldwin (2001) and Tierney and Readence (2000) provide examples of the PORPE strategy. Readers may also want to refer to Flippo (2000) for more extensive details and ideas for predicting, practicing, and answering essay exam questions and promoting students' independent learning and responsibility.

REAP

REAP is a four-step strategy designed by Eanet and Manzo (1976). This learning strategy is designed to enhance students' understanding, analysis of ideas, and thoughtful responses to content-area readings. Each step of REAP is described as follows:

1. *R—Read.* During this step, students are to read a textbook selection or part of a selection.

2. *E—Encode.* This step involves the students internalizing the information they have read and restating it in their own words. Students practice and rehearse this individually and privately.

3. *A—Annotate.* In this step, students react to the material they have read (and thought about—see the encode step) by writing a brief

Figure 6–2   Checklist for evaluating an essay exam response

	Yes	Somewhat	No
1. The question was answered completely. *Evaluation notes:*			
2. An introduction was provided that helped set up the answer. *Evaluation notes:*			
3. The essay was well organized with major points clearly stated. *Evaluation notes:*			
4. Important details or examples were provided to support each major point. *Evaluation notes:*			
5. The essay answer made sense and showed that the writer understood the material. *Evaluation notes:*			

explanation of their thinking and comments they want to make about the material.

4. *P—Ponder.* This step involves a discussion about the subject matter that was read and learned. The teacher instigates this, encouraging students to share, discuss, and explain their annotations with each other.

This procedure is continued with the next textbook segment to be read and studied. During each of the *ponder* steps, the teacher encourages the sharing of annotations and learning. Once the strategy is learned, the students can do the REAP procedure individually or in groups, whichever the teacher believes is most effective for the learning goals. Hayes (1992) provides examples of use of the REAP strategy.

SQ3R

This study strategy system was designed to help students develop an approach to previewing and reading their textbook chapters, and it is perhaps the most famous strategy system of all. Although it was designed by Robinson (back in 1946), it seems that new spin-offs of it appear regularly—most likely because it is so well known and tends to have wide applicability. In fact, you will probably notice similarities with some of the other strategy systems described in this chapter. As with all other strategy systems, it is important to realize that students need a lot of opportunities to practice with it for it to be used effectively.

There are five steps to SQ3R.

1. *S—Survey.* Students look over the entire chapter, briefly examining the title, headings, text, pictures, introduction, summary, etc., while asking themselves, "What is this chapter about?"

2. *Q—Question.* Next, students go back through the chapter and use each section heading to devise a question. It is suggested that stu-

dents write the questions. In the next step, they can be used to set a purpose for reading each section.

3. *R—Read.* Now students should actually read the entire chapter in order to try to answer the questions they posed. It is suggested that students take notes to answer their questions. (The chapter reading can be done silently, orally, individually, with the teacher, or with partners, at the teacher's discretion and also depending on the grade level of the students.)

4. *R—Recite.* Next the students are to recite the important information they noted from each section, again (as above) individually, with partners, or with the teacher.

5. *R—Review.* For this last step, students should be encouraged to review what they have read and their notes, and try to summarize the information into major points. Encourage them to write these points. Using the major points, try again to answer the question, "What is this chapter about?"

In my book *Assessing Readers* (2003), I include a teacher-developed lesson plan integrating the SQ3R procedure with the powerful dynamics of cooperative learning. For an illustration of how this can be done, see pages 332–34 in Flippo (2003).

PARS

This study-reading strategy developed by Smith and Elliot (1979) is particularly useful for elementary students with limited prior experience in using study-reading strategy techniques. The PARS steps to demonstrate and practice with students and then encourage them to use independently are as follows:

1. *Preview* the material to better understand its organization, that is, its important headings or concepts.

2. *Ask questions* before reading to help you understand the purpose or purposes inherent in your reading.

3. *Read* with those purpose-setting questions as a guide.

4. *Summarize* the reading by analyzing information gained against your questions.

SIP

Dana (1989) developed this study-reading strategy that is designed to help readers with special needs concentrate their attention on content while reading. It is effective with both narrative and expository text. The three steps for SIP are as follows:

1. *Summarize* the content of each page or naturally divided section of the text. This enables students to reflect on and interact with the text more effectively.

2. *Imaging* reminds the students to try to form an internal visual display of content encountered while reading. It also provides a second imprint of the text's content but is economical because it adds no time to the reading task.

3. *Predict* while reading. Students should try to pause after each page or naturally divided section in the text, reflect on the text, and predict what might happen next. During this step, students can verify, revise, or modify predictions based on what they have learned.

RIPS

Dana (1989) designed this study-reading strategy for readers with special needs to combat difficulties understanding text while reading. It is also effective in converting negative impressions toward the text material into more positive ones. The four steps of RIPS are as follows:

1. *Read on* and then *reread* when necessary. If comprehension deteriorates while reading, students should be encouraged to stop and reread until their understanding of the text improves.

2. *Imaging* is a crucial component of this strategy, and students are asked to visualize the content to provide themselves with an imprint of the material. Visual images that make no sense are an indication to students that comprehension difficulties are continuing.

3. *Paraphrase* those sections that are problem areas, and then ask students to try to restate the information in their own words.

4. *Speed up, slow down, and/or seek help.* Explain to students that during the "reading on" and "rereading" of text, they may need to speed up or slow down their rate of reading. When all else fails, students should seek your assistance for more modeling and scaffolding of the strategy system.

Inference Awareness

This reading and learning strategy was described by Gordon (1985) as a procedure to assist readers in locating information that is implied rather than directly stated in content materials. The five steps of this strategy are as follows:

1. Discuss with your students that in order to understand some text materials, readers must activate their own prior knowledge and experiences to understand what the writer intended but did not directly state.

2. In the second step, you model "inferencing" by reading a selection from the text material, then asking an inference question, giving

your own answer, and discussing with your students the cognitive processing involved.

3. The third step of this strategy involves a collaborative effort between you and your students. You ask and then answer another inference question, but in this step the students are asked to provide documentation that supports or refutes your answer. Encourage dialogue among your students and between your students and yourself.

4. During this step, students write the answers to the inference questions while you provide the supporting documentation; then, students and teacher discuss the responses and supporting documentation.

5. In the last step, students are responsible for locating the answers to the questions, finding supporting documentation, and explaining the cognitive processes involved.

Reflection Activity 6.1

How might you encourage your students to develop and use their own individual strategies for reading, studying, and learning? What rationale might you provide for this activity?

Strategy Systems for Reading, Studying, and Learning: A Summary

Learning how to learn is one of the most important things that a student can learn to do. Strategy systems can present an effective means of facilitating this learning. However, in order for study strategies and systems to be effective, students must have ample opportunities to practice using them with teacher support, as needed, and always with purposeful, authentic assignments. Additionally, all strategy systems will not necessarily be effective for all students, at all times, and under all conditions.

This chapter has presented strategies to help you and your students get started. There are literally hundreds of strategies for reading, studying, and learning that have been conceived over the years. Many are spin-offs of others. Teachers and students can develop their own strategies and spin-offs to fit their own needs, preferences, and the curricula to be learned. This *new* strategy development is to be encouraged.

1. After students have had many opportunities to have the Reciprocal Teaching and Learning strategy modeled for them and used in class, select a student teacher volunteer of the week (or month, or particular subject). Within an actual curricula area of the student's special interest, the student should be allowed to lead the class in learning by following the guidelines for Reciprocal Teaching and Learning. If this is successful and other students would like opportunities to be a "student teacher," then try it out again and again.

2. Would it be helpful to facilitate a discussion with your class or a small group of students as to what helps them with their reading, studying, and learning, and why? You could record all the ideas and methods they share on a chart and categorize them. (If the age of your class is too young to have enough studying experience, invite some children from a higher grade to have the discussion in front of the class.) You could ask students to evaluate the different ideas and methods listed on the chart. If they do not think an approach is "right" for them, you could ask them to explain why they feel this way.

3. After sufficient teacher modeling and scaffolding and student reading/studying/learning with a number of the strategy systems from this chapter, list the various strategies used by your class. Discuss as a class which strategies were most useful in which circumstances and how each strategy compares. In cooperative groups, allow students to create their own strategy for reading, studying, and learning. They can incorporate ideas from strategies already presented or think of their own. Allow students to practice on text with their new strategy and report to the class what their strategy is and how it helped them read or learn from text.

4. One or more of the above group-developed strategies could be used by the teacher or by a "student teacher" from the creating group to lead the class in the reading and/or learning of required school curricula.

Afterword

Study-learning skills and strategies enable students to pursue and accomplish the many assignments and study tasks they are given in school. They also provide students with the tools that they need to acquire and learn information from texts and other resources. Developing these skills and strategies is important to students "learning how to learn." Learning how to learn *should be* the goal of school instruction.

As teachers we owe it to our students to fulfill this goal: It is up to us to ensure that our students develop the studying and learning strategies they each need to enhance their independence and success as learners. It is never too soon to help students develop these strategies—from the primary grades on, *each teacher can help*.

Teachers using this book are to be congratulated on their dedication. The skills and strategies for studying and learning from text are often the "invisible" ones—that is, they are not typically at the forefront of politics and school reform movements—often they are an afterthought to the decision shapers and makers because they cannot be easily tested and documented. Nevertheless, *they are* really crucial to students' performance.

This book is but a primer for teachers. It is just a beginning point: Once you are dedicated to the idea of developing students' strategies for studying and learning from text, you will find many other ways to do it—over and above what has been presented in this little book. Just look to your own teaching expertise and know-how and you will be able to design many strategies and activities to fit your grade level, students' development and needs, your assignments, and specific curriculum demands. Good luck and thank you for your dedication and participation!

Rona Flippo

More Try It Out Activities

1. Ask your students to articulate verbally or in writing what is involved in "learning how to learn" and how it fits with their existing classroom work. Primary grade students could draw pictures to answer this question and then tell about the pictures. Older students might enjoy developing skits to demonstrate their points. Try it out.

2. Design your own scaffolded reading experience for your particular grade level. Include at least one prereading, during-reading, and postreading experience to fit a particular content study-learning unit of your choice. Try this out with students.

3. Design a study guide for reading, studying, and learning science-related material for your particular grade level. Try it out with students.

4. Design a different type of study guide for reading, studying, and learning history or other social-studies-related material for your particular grade level. Try it out with students.

5. In Reflection Activity 4.1, you focused on ideas for developing a reference and research skills assignment for elementary or middle school youngsters. Referring back to that, select one of your ideas and detail a lesson or activity for your students. Remember to use fading and to apply the assignment to authentic content learning. Try it out with students.

6. In Reflection Activity 4.2, you focused on ideas for developing the outlining, underlining, student glossing, and note-taking and note-making skills of elementary and middle school students. Referring back to that, select one of your ideas and detail a lesson or activity for students. Remember to use fading and to apply the assignment to authentic content learning. Try it out with students.

7. Develop an original lesson or activity for your grade level for enhancing one of the specialized study-learning skills described in this book. Remember to use fading and to apply the lesson to authentic content learning. Try it out with students.

8. Demonstrate, model, and scaffold some appropriate test-preparation and test-taking skills and strategies with your students. Help students apply these skills/strategies to real content materials and learning in your classroom. Try it out. How did it go?

9. Select one of the strategy systems for reading, studying, and learning from text. Show your students how to use the selected strategy. Use the teaching techniques of demonstrating, modeling, scaffolding, and fading to help students read, study, learn, and apply the strategy to real content material. Try it out. How did it go?

10. Help students to feel confident about the information they have learned by giving them the opportunity to *show* they have learned it through alternative means, other than tests. For example, using some of the strategy systems presented in Chapter 6 (K-W-L, or a variation; Reciprocal Teaching and Learning; Predict-Test-Conclude; Think-Alouds; PORPE; REAP; SQ3R; PARS; SIP; RIPS; and Inference Awareness), allow students to *demonstrate* what they have learned. These strategy systems for reading, studying, and learning promote metacognitive thinking, and observing students' metacognitive thinking/awareness is an excellent way of assessing their comprehension of material. Try it out. How did it go?

11. Look for ways to deepen understanding of expository reading assignments by having students focus on the purpose of the reading. Consider asking the following questions during class discussion after a chapter has been read:

- What was the purpose of this reading assignment?
- Where is this discussion taking us and why is it important?
- How does what we just read in this chapter fit in with what we have learned so far?
- Does it change the direction of what we've learned?
- Does it fit the pattern of what we know already?

Try it out.

12. Create an ongoing study-learning activity center in your classroom. After modeling and providing practice with a number of study guides, have students rotate through a number of guides for different learning tasks. Make sure students know the criteria for each task, including specific information they will be responsible for, questions they need to answer, and how they will be assessed. At the end of each study-learning task ask students to reflect on how the guide they used was a help or hindrance in their learning. Try it out.

13. Create a grid or a display chart for your classroom of the study and learning strategies you've successfully used with your students. With their input, indicate or check off next to each strategy when or how it would be most useful. Brainstorm with your students other ideas that would be helpful in studying and learning and list them. Many students will find that this classroom chart is a helpful reminder for future use of these strategies. Try it out.

14. Ask students to think about the various study and learning strategies that they have been using in class. Would they take a few moments to reflect about this in their journals?

    - Which strategies have been the most effective toward helping them learn?
    - Which strategy helped them understand and remember the most?

    Try it out.

15. As an extension of the above, or on its own, have students list the steps they took in using their preferred learning strategy.

    - Which steps were the easiest to use?
    - How did they help you learn the material?

    Try it out.

16. With students in your classroom, design study guides, study-learning strategies, test-preparation strategies, or other strategies that you and your students believe would be helpful for reading, studying, and learning from text. Encourage students to design their own. Students can name their strategies after themselves or any other name that they think "fits." For example, "John's Strategy" or "How to Succeed

in Outlining the Most Important Information Strategy" (HSOMIIS).
Let students try them out and discuss their successes. How did it go?

17. Have your students create study guides for younger students to use in their learning as part of a cross-age tutoring experience. Try it out.

18. Have students model for peers in other classrooms or younger students how to take notes from text using note-taking techniques learned in class. Try it out.

19. Frequently give students opportunities to use electronic research sources as well as printed sources. For instance, for Mrs. Argueta's assignment, students could have done the following:

   - downloaded a map from the Web showing the location of the world's rainforests
   - used email to contact conservation and other special interest groups in the regions of each rainforest to ask specific questions and to get the most up-to-date information
   - compared that information with various print sources found in the library to evaluate how things might have changed (and possibly further deteriorated or improved) since the publications of those print sources

   Try it out.

20. Frequently give students opportunities to showcase their learnings. Students could

   - publish, bind, and illustrate (or scan pictures) to share their reports and other information
   - prepare and show PowerPoint presentations of their learnings
   - post their reports on the Web on an educational site
   - share their learnings with peers in their class or other classes, parents and family members during special programs, and interested younger grade children or senior citizen groups

   Try it out.

Appendix of Studying and Learning Forms

Assignment Analysis Sheet

1. Specific assignment or learning: _____
   _____
   _____
   _____

2. Authentic purpose(s) for assignment or learning: _____
   _____
   _____
   _____

3. Steps students will need to take in order to complete this assignment and learning: _____
   _____
   _____
   _____
   _____

4. Specific study skills and strategies needed to complete each step: _____
   _____
   _____
   _____
   _____

5. How this assignment or learning will be evaluated: _____
   _____
   _____
   _____
   _____

6. What is my exact criteria and requirements for this assignment or learning? _____
   _____
   _____
   _____
   _____
   _____
   _____

Study Skills and Strategies

Students' names:	Planning and organizing	Library and Internet research	Skimming and scanning	Adjusting rate	Using graphic information	Note taking	Outlining	Summarizing	Report writing	Editing	Using dictionary	Oral reporting	Notes:

Think-Through "To Do" Sheet

What I have to do:	Check when it is done:
The order I should do it in:	
When I should do it:	

Think-Through "How To Do" Sheet

I have to...	Do I know how to?	Where I can get help...
(List study skills you have to use below	(Yes, No, Maybe)	(From the teacher, librarian, friend, family, etc.)

Student Reflection Guide

1. Did I complete the study or learning assignments as explained by the teacher? (To be sure, compare the teacher's criteria to your work and see if it is complete or finished.)

2. What kind of grade or evaluation do I think I will get on this assignment, activity, or test? Why?

3. Is there something else I could do to get a better grade or evaluation on it? What?

4. Do I have the time to do more to get the better grade? How much more time do I need? Will it be worth it?

5. What did I learn from this study or assignment? Is this what the teacher was expecting me to learn? Is there something else I can do to learn more or to meet the teacher's criteria? Am I willing to do it? Why or why not?

6. Overall, am I satisfied with my learning or work? Why or why not? If not, how can I improve it?

Class or Unit: _____   Date: _____

General Topic _____

Subtopic _____   Notes: _____

_____

_____

_____

_____

_____

_____

_____

_____

_____

_____

New Subtopic _____   Notes: _____

_____

_____

_____

_____

_____

_____

_____

_____

_____

_____

New Subtopic _____   Notes: _____

_____

_____

_____

_____

_____

_____

_____

_____

_____

_____

_____

K-W-L-WN-W

Topic: _____

Goal: _____

_____

K What I know:	W What do I want to learn?	L What I learned:	WN What now do I still want to/need to learn?	W Where can I find the additional information?

	Yes	Somewhat	No
1. The question was answered completely. *Evaluation notes:*			
2. An introduction was provided that helped set up the answer. *Evaluation notes:*			
3. The essay was well organized with major points clearly stated. *Evaluation notes:*			
4. Important details or examples were provided to support each major point. *Evaluation notes:*			
5. The essay answer made sense and showed that the writer understood the material. *Evaluation notes:*			

References

Allgood, W. P., J. Risko, M. C. Alvarez, and M. M. Fairbanks. 2000. "Factors that Influence Study." In *Handbook of College Reading and Study Strategy Research*, edited by R. F. Flippo and D. C. Caverly, 201–19. Mahwah, NJ: Erlbaum.

Alvermann, D. E., and S. F. Phelps. 2002. *Content Reading and Literacy: Succeeding in Today's Diverse Classrooms*, 3d ed. Boston: Allyn and Bacon.

Anderson, R. C., E. H. Hiebert, J. A. Scott, and I. A. G. Wilkinson. 1985. *Becoming a Nation of Readers*. Washington, DC: National Institute of Education.

Anderson, T. H., and B. B. Armbruster. 1984. "Studying." In *Handbook of Reading Research*, edited by P. D. Pearson, R. Barr, M. L. Kamil, and P. Mosenthal, 657–79. New York: Longman.

Armbruster, B. B. 2000. "Taking Notes from Lectures." In *Handbook of College Reading and Strategy Research*, edited by R. F. Flippo and D. C. Caverly, 175–99. Mahwah, NJ: Erlbaum.

Armbruster, B. B., and J. O. Armstrong. 1993. "Locating Information in Text: A Focus on Children." *Contemporary Educational Psychology* 18: 139–61.

Baker, L., and A. L. Brown. 1984. "Metacognitive Skills and Reading." In *Handbook of Reading Research*, edited by P. D. Pearson, R. Barr, M. L. Kamil, and P. Mosenthal, 353–94. New York: Longman.

Baker, R. L. 1977. "The Effects of Inferential Organizers on Learning and Retention, Content Knowledge, and Term Relationships in Ninth Grade Social Studies." In *Research in Reading in the Content Areas: The Third Report*, edited by H. L. Herber and R. T. Vacca. Syracuse, NY: Syracuse University Reading and Language Arts Center.

Bandura, A. 1993. "Perceived Self-Efficacy in Cognitive Development and Functioning." *Educational Psychologist* 28(2): 117–48.

Bean, T. W., H. Singer, and S. Cowan. 1985. "Analogical Study Guides: Improving Comprehension in Science." *Journal of Reading* 29: 246–50.

Bereiter, C., and M. Scardamalia. 1987. "An Attainable Version of High Literacy: Approaches to Teaching Higher-Order Skills in Reading and Writing." *Curriculum Inquiry 17*(1): 9–30.

Blanchard, J. S. 1985. "What to Tell Students about Underlining . . . and Why." *Journal of Reading* 29: 199–203.

Borkowski, J. G., M. Carr, E. Rellinger, and M. Pressley. 1990. "Self-Regulated Cognition: Interdependence of Metacognition, Attribution, and Self-Esteem." In *Dimensions of Thinking and Cognitive Instruction,* edited by B. F. Jones and L. Idol, 53–92. Hillsdale, NJ: Erlbaum.

Brophy, J. 1986. "Teacher Influences on Student Achievement." *American Psychologist* 41: 1069–77.

Caverly, D. C., V. P. Orlando, and J. L. Mullen. 2000. "Textbook Study Reading." In *Handbook of College Reading and Study Strategy Research,* edited by R. F. Flippo and D. C. Caverly, 105–47. Mahwah, NJ: Erlbaum.

Cole, J., and K. Gardner. 1979. "Topic Work with First-Year Secondary Pupils." In *The Effective Use of Reading,* edited by E. Lunzer and K. Gardner, 167–92. London: Heinemann.

Cramer, E. H., and M. Castle, editors. 1994. *Fostering the Love of Reading: The Affective Domain in Reading Education.* Newark, DE: International Reading Association.

Dana, C. 1989. "Strategy Families for Disabled Readers." *Journal of Reading* 33: 31–32.

Dansereau, D. F. 1985. "Learning Strategy Theory." In *Thinking and Learning Skills: Vol. 1: Relating Instruction to Research,* edited by J. W. Segal, S. W. Chipman, and R. Glaser, 209–39. Hillsdale, NJ: Erlbaum.

Devine, T. G. 1987. *Teaching Study Skills: A Guide for Teachers,* 2d ed. Boston: Allyn and Bacon.

Devine, T. G., and J. S. Kania. 2003. "Studying: Skills, Strategies, and Systems." In *Handbook of Research on Teaching the English Language Arts,* 2d ed., edited by J. Flood, D. Lapp, J. R. Squire, and J. M. Jensen, 942–54. Mahwah, NJ: Erlbaum.

Dole, J. A., G. G. Duffy, L. R. Roehler, and P. D. Pearson. 1991. "Moving from the Old to the New: Research on Reading Comprehension Instruction." *Review of Educational Research 61*(2): 239–64.

Dreher, M. J. 1993. "Reading to Locate Information: Societal and Educational Perspectives." *Contemporary Education Psychology* 18: 129–38.

Dreher, M. J., and R. B. Sammons. 1994. "Fifth Graders' Search for Information in a Textbook." *Journal of Reading Behavior 26*(2): 301–14.

Dreher, M. J., and W. H. Slater. 1992. "Elementary School Literacy: Critical Issues." In *Elementary School Literacy: Critical Issues,* edited by M. J. Dreher and W. H. Slater, 3–25. Norwood, MA: Christopher-Gordon.

Duffelmeyer, F. A. 1994. "Effective Anticipation Guide Statements for Learning from Expository Prose." *Journal of Reading 37*(6): 452–57.

Duffelmeyer, F. A., D. D. Baum, and D. J. Merkley. 1987. "Maximizing Reader-Text Confrontation with an Extended Anticipation Guide." *Journal of Reading* 31: 146–50.

Dwyer, E. J., and E. E. Dwyer. 1994. "How Teachers' Attitudes Influence Reading Achievement." In *Fostering the Love of Reading: The Affective Domain in Reading Education,* edited by E. H. Cramer and M. Castle, 66–73. Newark, DE: International Reading Association.

Eanet, M., and A. V. Manzo. 1976. "REAP—A Strategy for Improving Reading/Writing/Discussion Skills." *Journal of Reading* 19, 647–52.

Flippo, R. F. 2003. *Assessing Readers: Qualitative Diagnosis and Instruction.* Portsmouth, NH: Heinemann.

———. 2002. "Study Skills and Strategies." In *Literacy in America: An Encyclopedia of History, Theory, and Practice,* Vol. 2, edited by B. Guzzetti, 631–32. Santa Barbara, CA: ABC-CLIO.

———. 2000. *TestWise: Strategies for Success in Taking Tests,* 2d ed. Grand Rapids, MI: Good Apple an imprint of McGraw-Hill Children's Publishing.

Flippo, R. F., M. J. Becker, and D. M. Wark. 2000. "Preparing for and Taking Tests." In *Handbook of College Reading and Study Strategy Research,* edited by R. F. Flippo and D. C. Caverly, 221–60. Mahwah, NJ: Erlbaum.

Flippo, R. F., and P. Borthwick. 1982. "Should Testwiseness Curriculum Be a Part of Undergraduate Teacher Education?" In *Reading in the Disciplines, Second Yearbook of the American Reading Forum,* edited by G. H. McNinch, 117–20. Athens, GA: American Reading Forum.

Flippo, R. F., and C. R. Frounfelker III. 1988. "Teach Map Reading Through Self Assessment." *The Reading Teacher 42*(3): 259.

Flippo, R. F., and R. L. Lecheler. 1987. "Adjusting Reading Rate: Metacognitive Awareness." *The Reading Teacher 40*(7): 712–13.

Fry, E. B. 1989. *Skimming & Scanning: Intermediate Level,* 2d ed. Providence, RI: Jamestown.

———. 1981. "Graphical Literacy." *Journal of Reading* 24: 383–89.

Good, T. L., and J. Brophy. 1978. *Looking in Classrooms.* New York: Harper-Collins.

Gordon, C. J. 1985. "Modeling Inference Awareness Across the Curriculum." *Journal of Reading 28*(5): 444–47.

Graves, M., and B. Graves. 2003. *Scaffolding Reading Experiences: Designs for Student Success,* 2d ed. Norwood, MA: Christopher-Gordon.

Guthrie, J. T. 1994. "Creating Interest in Reading." *Reading Today 12*(l): 24.

Guthrie, J. T., and M. Pressley. 1992. "Reading as Cognition and the Mediation of Experience." In *Elementary School Literacy: Critical Issues,* edited by M. J. Dreher and W. H. Slater, 241–60. Norwood, MA: Christopher-Gordon.

Guthrie, J. T., and A. Wigfield. 2000. "Engagement and Motivation in Reading." In *Handbook of Reading Research,* Vol. III, edited by M. Kamil, P. B. Mosenthal, P. D. Pearson, and R. Barr, 403–22. Mahwah, NJ: Erlbaum.

Harris, A. J., and E. R. Sipay. 1990. *How to Increase Reading Ability: A Guide to Developmental and Remedial Methods,* 9th ed. New York: Longman.

Hayes, D. A. 1992. *A Sourcebook of Interactive Methods for Teaching with Texts.* Boston: Allyn and Bacon.

Heller, M. F. 1986. "How Do You Know What You Know? Metacognitive Modeling in the Content Areas." *Journal of Reading 29*(5):415–22.

Herber, H. L. 1978. *Teaching Reading in Content Areas.* Englewood Cliffs, NJ: Prentice-Hall.

Hoyt, L. 2002. *Make it Real: Strategies for Success with Informational Texts.* Portsmouth, NH: Heinemann.

Hyde, A. A., and M. Bizar. 1996. *Thinking in Context: Teaching Cognitive Processes Across the Elementary School Curriculum,* 2d ed. New York: Longman.

Johnston, P. 1985. "Teaching Students to Apply Strategies That Improve Reading Comprehension." The *Elementary School Journal 8*(5): 635–44.

Kauchak, D. P., and P. D. Eggen. 2003. *Learning and Teaching: Research-Based Methods,* 4th ed. Boston: Allyn and Bacon.

Kiewra, K. A. 1984. "Acquiring Effective Notetaking Skills: An Alternative to Professional Notetaking." *Journal of Reading 27*: 299–302.

Klein, M. L. 1988. *Teaching Reading Comprehension and Vocabulary,* 39–46. Englewood Cliffs, NJ: Prentice-Hall.

Kucan, L., and I. L. Beck. 1997. "Thinking Aloud and Reading Comprehension Research: Inquiry, Instruction, and Social Interaction." *Review of Educational Research 67*: 271–99.

Levin, J. R. 1976. "What Have We Learned About Maximizing What Children Learn?" In *Cognitive Learning in Children: Theories and Strategies,* edited by J. R. Levin and V. L. Allen. New York: Academic Press.

Mandeville, T. L. 1994. "KWLA: Linking the Affective and Cognitive Domains." *The Reading Teacher 17*(8): 679–80.

Maxim, G. W. 2003. *Dynamic Social Studies for Elementary Classrooms,* 7th ed. Upper Saddle River, NJ: Merrill/Prentice-Hall.

McAndrew, D. A. 1983. "Underlining and Notetaking: Some Suggestions for Research." *Journal of Reading* 27: 103–08.

McCabe, P. P. 1984. "Stretch Your Budgets: Have Schools and Public Libraries Cooperate." *Journal of Reading* 27: 632–35.

McKenna, M. C., and R. D. Robinson. 2002. *Teaching Through Text: Reading and Writing in the Content Areas,* 3d ed. Boston: Allyn and Bacon.

Mier, M. 1984. "Comprehension Monitoring in One Elementary Classroom." *The Reading Teacher 37*(8): 770–74.

Miller, M. J. 1979. "The Primary Child in the Library." In *Developing Active Readers: Ideas for Parents, Teachers, and Librarians,* edited by L. Monson and D. McClenathan. Newark, DE: International Reading Association.

Moore, D. W., S. A. Moore, P. M. Cunningham, and J. W. Cunningham. 2003. *Developing Readers and Writers in the Content Areas K–12,* 4th ed. Boston: Allyn and Bacon.

Nelson, R. M. 1973. "Getting Children into Reference Books." *Elementary English* 50: 884–86.

Ogle, D. M. 1986. "K-W-L: A Teaching Model That Develops Active Reading of Expository Text." *The Reading Teacher* 39: 564–70.

Otto, W., S. White, D. Richgels, R. Hansen, and B. Morrison. 1981. *A Technique for Improving the Understanding of Expository Text: Gloss and Examples* (Theoretical Paper No. 96). Madison, WI: Wisconsin Center for Education Research.

Palincsar, A. S., and A. L. Brown. 1984. "Reciprocal Teaching of Comprehension-Fostering and Comprehension-Monitoring Activities." *Cognition and Instruction* 1: 117–75.

Palincsar, A. S., and A. L. Brown. 1986. "Interactive Teaching to Promote Independent Learning from Text." *The Reading Teacher* 29: 771–77.

Paris, S. G., B. A. Wasik, and J. C. Turner. 1991. "The Development of Strategic Readers." In *Handbook of Reading Research,* Vol. II, edited by R. Barr, M. Kamil, P. B. Mosenthal, and P. D. Pearson, 609–40. New York: Longman.

Paris, S. G., and P. Winograd. 1990. "How Metacognition Can Promote Academic Learning and Instruction." In *Dimensions of Thinking and Cognitive Instruction,* edited by B. F. Jones and L. Idol, 16–51. Hillsdale, NJ: Erlbaum.

Pauk, W. 2001. *How to Study in College,* 7th ed. Boston: Houghton Mifflin.

Pearson, P. D., and L. Fielding. 1991. "Comprehension Instruction." In *Handbook of Reading Research,* Vol. II, edited by R. Barr, M. Kamil, P. B. Mosenthal, and P. D. Pearson, 815–60. New York: Longman.

Poostay, E. J. 1984. "Show Me Your Underlines: A Strategy to Teach Comprehension." *The Reading Teacher* 37: 828–30.

Readence, J. E., T. W. Bean, and R. S. Baldwin. 2001. *Content Area Literacy: An Integrated Approach,* 7th ed. Dubuque, IA: Kendall/Hunt.

Robb, L. 2003. *Teaching Reading in Social Studies, Science, and Math.* New York: Scholastic.

Robinson, F. P. 1946. *Effective Study.* New York: Harper and Brothers.

Roehler, L. R., and G. G. Duffy. 1991. "Teachers' Instructional Actions." In *Handbook of Reading Research,* Vol. II, edited by R. Barr, M. Kamil, P. B. Mosenthal, and P. D. Pearson, 861–83. New York: Longman.

Ruddell, R. B. 2002. *Teaching Children to Read and Write: Becoming an Effective Literacy Teacher,* 3d ed. Boston: Allyn and Bacon.

Rumelhart, D. E. 1980. "Schemata: The Building Blocks of Cognition." In *Theoretical Issues in Reading Comprehension,* edited by R. J. Spiro, B. C. Bruce, and W. F. Brewer, 33–58. Hillsdale, NJ: Erlbaum.

Salend, S. J. 2001. *Creating Inclusive Classrooms: Effective Mainstreaming,* 4th ed. Upper Saddle River, NJ: Merrill/Prentice-Hall.

Shepherd, J. F. 1998. *College Study Skills,* 6th ed. Boston: Houghton Mifflin.

Simpson, M. L. 1984. "The Status of Study Strategy Instruction: Implications for Classroom Teachers." *Journal of Reading* 28: 136–43.

Simpson, M. L., N. A. Stahl, and C. G. Hayes. 1989. "PORPE: A Research Validation." *Journal of Reading* 33: 22–29.

Sivertsen, M. L. 1993. *State of the Art: Transforming Ideas for Teaching and Learning Science.* Washington, DC: Office of Research, U.S. Department of Education.

Slavin, R. E. 1995. *Cooperative Learning,* 2d ed. Boston: Allyn and Bacon.

———. 1987. *Cooperative Learning: Student Teams,* 2d ed. Washington, DC: National Education Association.

Smith, C. B., and P. G. Elliot. 1979. *Reading Activities for Middle and Secondary Schools.* New York: Holt, Rinehart & Winston.

Taylor, B. M. 2002. "Peer and Cross-Age Tutoring." In *Literacy in America: An Encyclopedia of History, Theory, and Practice,* Vol. 2, edited by B. Guzzetti, 419–20. Santa Barbara, CA: ABC-CLIO.

Tierney, R. J. 1982. "Essential Considerations for Developing Basic Reading Comprehension Skills." *School Psychology Review* 11(3): 299–305.

Tierney, R. J., and J. E. Readence. 2000. *Reading Strategies and Practices: A Compendium,* 5th ed. Boston: Allyn and Bacon.

Turner, J. C., and S. G. Paris. 1995. "How Literacy Tasks Influence Children's Motivation for Literacy." *The Reading Teacher 48*(8): 662–73.

Wade, S. E., and R. E. Reynolds. 1989. "Developing Metacognitive Awareness." *Journal of Reading* 33: 6–14.

Weinstein, C. E., and E. Mayer. 1986. "The Teaching of Learning Strategies." In *Handbook of Research on Teaching,* 3d ed., edited by M. C. Wittrock, 315–17. New York: Macmillan.

Wharton-MacDonald, R., M. Pressley, and J. M. Hampston. 1998. "Literacy Instruction in Nine First-Grade Classrooms: Teacher Characteristics and Student Achievement." *The Elementary School Journal 99*(2): 101–28.

Wood, K. D. 1988. "Guiding Students through Informational Text." *The Reading Teacher 41*(9): 912–20.

Wood, K. D., D. Lapp, and J. Flood. 1992. *Guiding Readers Through Text: A Review of Study Guides.* Newark, DE: International Reading Association.

Zemelman, S., and H. Daniels. 1988. *A Community of Writers.* Portsmouth, NH: Heinemann.